Decorative Cakes

Rosemary Wadey · Janice Murfitt

Contents

Note
1. All spoon measurements are level. Spoon measures can be bought in both imperial and metric sizes to give accurate measurement of small quantities.
2. All eggs are size 2 unless otherwise stated.
3. All sugar is granulated unless otherwise stated.
4. Preparation times given are an average calculated during recipe testing.
5. Metric and imperial measurements have been calculated separately. Use one set of measurements only as they are not exact equivalents.
6. Cooking times may vary slightly depending on the individual oven. Dishes should be placed in the centre of an oven unless otherwise specified.
7. Always preheat the oven to the specified temperature.
8. If using a fan-assisted oven, follow the manufacturer's instructions for guidance on temperature adjustments.

This edition published in 1989
by The Hamlyn Publishing Group,
a division of the Octopus Publishing Group,
Michelin House,
81 Fulham Road,
London SW3 6RB

Copyright © 1986 Hennerwood Publications Limited

ISBN 0 600 56454 1

Produced by Mandarin Offset.
Printed and bound in Hong Kong.

Introduction

For many of the big occasions in our lives, an elegant, wonderfully decorated cake forms the centre piece of the celebration, whether it be a christening, birthday party or wedding, or an event like Christmas. As this book shows, the creation of the cake does not have to be a task for the professional, but can be achieved successfully at home.

Decorating cakes is an art which is ever increasing in popularity. This book aims to take you through the basics, on to the simpler decorating techniques. From there it progresses to more advanced decoration, giving you a chance to show off your newly acquired skills. Chapter 4 looks at other forms of cake decoration with some superb continental gâteaux. This leads to the novelty cakes which combine many of the techniques of the previous chapters to produce fantastic creations of like appeal to adults and children. Finally there is a section of small cakes and biscuits as smaller scale examples of the decorator's art.

The First Steps

The first essential step in all cake decorating is to be able to make a good basic cake, whether a simple quick mix or a more elaborate fruit cake. After all, if you are going to spend a lot of time on the icing and decoration of the cake, the base should be really good to eat as well. With many of the cakes a layer of marzipan is necessary to separate the cake from the icing and to prevent the grease from the cake seeping through on to the icing. It is important to get a good shape at this stage, to make it as easy as possible to add a smooth layer of icing.

Time and patience are the most important qualities for the student of cake decorating. A steady hand in its own right makes sense too, but this can be acquired with practice. The novelty cakes also take time and inspiration to build before even attempting the actual decoration.

The next step is to coat the cake with the base icing. This is added in various forms, depending on the particular type used and for a really good effect it is essential to achieve as flat a surface as possible and that only comes with practice. Remember that with any icing and especially with the more complicated designs, it is very important to read through the whole recipe first. Most decorated cakes will take several days to complete and many of the extra decorations should have been made well in advance to give them time to dry completely before they can be used and attached to the cake. In fact some can be made several weeks before required and will not deteriorate in any way provided they are kept in the dry in an airtight container. These decorations, particularly those made from royal icing, are always fragile, so it is wise to make at least 10-20 extra of the small ones, such as fans, and two or three extra of the large run-out figures and collars as reserves in case of mishap. A pair of tweezers is the best implement to use for moving them about most easily. If made in advance icing decorations should be allowed to dry completely, then packed in rigid containers between several layers of tissue paper or absorbent kitchen paper.

In The Beginning

If you are a beginner, try out some of the simpler designs first, gradually working up to those which are more complicated, as your skills increase. It is not necessary to try everything on the cake at first, in fact it is wiser to try a new design or process on something other than the cake first. You can practise on an upturned cake tin or any flat working surface, to prevent marking the flat surface you have prepared by making mistakes.

When modelling, take care to colour the moulding icing or marzipan really smoothly and to the desired colour. The separate colours required can be prepared before you begin and each stored in separate sealed polythene bags until required. Give your hands a good wash in between each colour to prevent

Preparatory steps
First decide on the type of cake you want, its decorations and colour scheme. Next, work out the time schedule for making and baking the cake, adding marzipan with time for it to dry, and icing the cake, allowing plenty of time for decoration. If it is a rich cake with elaborate decoration, try to have the cake completed 2 or 3 days before required; if a sponge cake, gâteau or small cakes, leave them as late as possible so they are at their freshest. Check you have all the correct ingredients before you begin.

any stains from transferring to other colours. To prevent the models from sticking to your fingers as you make them, dip your fingers in a mixture of icing sugar and cornflour, which will not in fact leave any taste but makes everything simpler to handle. These models are delightful for children's and novelty cakes and although they are edible, may well not be eaten, but kept as ornaments. The numerous types of icing flowers, however, which enhance so many cakes will probably be consumed when the cake is cut, although these flowers, too, will keep for an indefinite period; it is a tradition for many decorations from a wedding cake to be used on the first christening cake.

Confidence is a great asset particularly when it comes to creating elaborately-iced cakes, whether formal or novelty, so give it a go and watch your skills develop and the results improve with each new cake or decoration you attempt.

Basic Icing and Decorating Equipment

It is essential to have all the items necessary for cake icing and decorating gathered together before you start. Icing does not take kindly to being left whilst you dash out to buy a forgotten nozzle or icing comb. Some things are everyday kitchen items but others are more specialized and may have to be obtained from cake decorating shops (see page 144) or good hardware stores. Store the items carefully, so that they don't get damaged; a chip out of an icing ruler will always leave a dent in the icing when used; a bent nozzle will always result in uneven lines.

It is advisable always to buy the best quality equipment available; it will last well and should not rust, bend out of shape or chip in awkward places.

If possible keep some equipment especially for making icing. For instance, wooden spoons and plastic basins pick up flavours from strongly-flavoured foods and get stained too. Wooden spoons are better than metal

spoons for making and beating royal icing and preferable to using a mixer. Although a mixer makes the task easier, it produces far too many air bubbles, which are difficult to disperse and can ruin the flat surface of a cake if not carefully removed.

Stainless steel and plastic icing rulers are available in various lengths. They should be firm enough to keep straight but slightly flexible to help keep the icing smooth as the ruler is drawn across the cake. Practice will soon teach you how much pressure to use when doing this. A serrated plastic ruler is also available and can be used on both royal icing and butter cream to obtain a serrated topping.

The sides of a cake can be smoothed with a palette knife but a plastic icing comb or scraper makes the job much easier. They produce perfectly smooth sides and sharp corners, or, in the case of a serrated-edged comb, interesting wavy designs. It is easiest to use an icing comb if you have an icing turntable to swivel the cake at a regulated pace as the comb or scraper is pulled round the sides. For the beginner, an upturned plate or a simple turntable will suffice, but as you advance it is wise to invest in a really good one. It doesn't matter whether it is plastic or metal but it should be one that is heavy enough to take any size of cake and should swivel easily and smoothly at the touch of a finger. Whether it is a high- or low-standing one is a matter of preference.

Equipment for the Cake Decorator

The following is a list of basic items needed by the cake decorator:
a selection of bowls and basins (china or glass)
large and small measuring jugs
set of measuring spoons
tablespoons and teaspoons
nylon or good metal sieves
wooden spoons
spatulas
pastry brush
kitchen scissors
large and small palette knife/spreader or a round-bladed knife
icing ruler
icing comb or scraper (for the sides of the cakes)
skewers
string
rolling pin
wooden cocktail sticks
small bowls or containers with airtight seals
greaseproof paper, non-stick silicone or waxed paper and foil
selection of basic icing nozzles including fine, medium and thick writing, small, medium and large star, rosette, ribbon, small petal and leaf
tweezers
selection of liquid food colourings.

As your interest grows and you become more skilful, you may want to add the following to your icing equipment:
icing turntable
icing nail
metal or plastic templates
pair of compasses and/or cake markers
fine paint brushes.

Cake Tins

Cake tins for large, heavy rich cakes should be of a good quality, firm metal which will hold its shape and not dent during storage. Buy the sizes you are most likely to use first, then gradually collect others as you need them until you have a set of graduated sizes from 12.5-15 cm (5-6 inches) upwards to 30 cm (12 inches) or larger; and in both round and square shapes.

Many cakes are now made into other shapes and there are tins of all shapes and sizes available for these. Popular shapes include hexagonal, octagonal, heart, oval, petal, rectangular and horseshoe. These tins are also available in graduated sizes but can be hired at a minimal charge if only needed once for a special occasion. Shaped cakes can, however, be created by cutting round or square cakes (see opposite). In this way you can create any shape you fancy for your own special cake. An assortment of cake boards for other than round or square cakes is available but the choice is not very great so you may have to choose a round or square nearest the shape or cut out your own from several thicknesses of card, then cover with a thick special paper of silver or gold to make it look authentic.

Cake tins can be non-stick or otherwise but do ensure that for square tins the corners are really square. If not it is difficult to get a true square edge to the cake unless you build it up with marzipan before adding the icing. Older cake tins tended to measure a little less than the supposed size but modern ones can measure up to 5 mm (¼ inch) larger than the stated size. It is important to remember this when buying the boards and also to realise that the cooking time for a slightly larger tin may need to be reduced by about 15 minutes and the cake will be slightly shallower.

It is possible to buy cake tins with loose bases, making it very easy to remove the cakes, especially some of the softer gâteau types. Some of the tins are spring release; others are rigid tins with bases which just push up.

Lining Cake Tins

If using special non-stick tins, follow the manufacturer's instructions. With all other tins it is necessary either to grease and flour, or grease and line with greaseproof paper and grease again. Use oil, melted lard or melted margarine for greasing. If you wish to use non-stick silicone or waxed paper, there is no need to grease the paper. The cake tin, whether plain or with a non-stick coating, must be scrupulously cleaned before it is lined.

To Line a Shallow Rectangular Tin

1. Cut a piece of greaseproof about 7.5 cm (3 inches) larger than the tin, and larger still if the sides of the tin are deeper than 2.5 cm (1 inch).
2. Place the tin on the paper and make a cut from the corners of the paper to the corners of the tin.
3. Grease inside the tin, put in the paper, so that it fits neatly, overlapping the paper at the corners to give sharp angles, and grease again.

To Double Line a Deep Tin

1. For a round tin cut one or two strips of double greaseproof long enough to reach round the outside of the tin with enough to overlap, and wide enough to come 2.5 cm (1 inch) above the rim of the tin. Fold the bottom edge up about 2 cm (¾ inch) and crease it firmly. Open out and make slanting cuts into the folded strip at 2 cm (¾ inch) intervals.
2. Place the tin on a double thickness of greaseproof and draw round the base, then cut it out a little inside the line.
3. Grease the inside of the tin, place one paper circle in the base and grease just round the edge of the paper.
4. Place the long strips in the tin, pressing them against the sides with the cut edges spread over the base. Grease all over the side paper.
5. Finally position the second circle in the base and grease again.
6. For a square tin, follow the instructions for the deep round tin but make folds into the corners of the long strips.

Cutting the lining paper to fit a shallow rectangular tin

Fitting the lining paper into the greased shallow tin

Cutting the lining paper for a deep square tin

Positioning the second base paper in a deep square tin

Making special shapes

Cakes made in shapes different from the traditional round or square give opportunities for some different decoration styles as well. It is not necessary to have specially designed cake tins, either; round or square cakes can be adapted without difficulty to numerous shapes.

To Make a Horseshoe-Shaped Cake

Begin with a round cake and, using a paper pattern, first cut out a central circle of cake of 7.5-9 cm (3-3½ inches), then cut out a wedge-shaped piece evenly to complete the horseshoe.

A horse-shoe shaped cake in this book is the Congratulations Cake on page 47.

To Make a Petal-Shaped Cake

A petal cake can be cut from a slightly larger 23 cm (9 inch) round cake. First draw a template using a pair of compasses to get it quite even; then place on the cake and, using a sharp knife, cut out the scallops taking it right down to the base. Trim up until quite even. It will need a thicker than usual layer of apricot glaze to keep the crumbs of cake in place.

A petal-shaped cake in this book is the Christening Cake on page 46.

To Make An Oval-Shaped Cake

Select an oval glass dish whose length matches the diameter of the round cake you have made. Using this as a pattern, place on top of the cake and cut all around it with a sharp knife, keeping the sides straight. Alternatively, draw an oval shape the size you require on a piece of card and cut around this.

An oval-shaped cake in this book is the Engagement Cake on pages 58-9.

To Make a Heart-Shaped Cake

Begin with a round cake. Cut a heart-shaped paper pattern. The 'V' should be about 4 cm (1½ inches) deep on a 20 cm (8 inch) round cake and gradually deeper on larger cakes. The piece taken out should then be cut in half,

reversed and put at the other end of the cake to make a point. You will need to trim off a small triangular piece to make a good fit. Attach to the cake with apricot glaze or butter cream.

Heart-shaped cakes in this book are the Basket of Chocolates and the Heart-shaped Birthday Cake on pages 42-3.

To Make a Hexagonal-Shaped Cake

Take a compass and measure the length from the centre of the cake to the edge. Make a mark on the edge. Using the same measurement, position the compass point at the mark on the edge and make another mark with the other end, also on the edge. Continue in this way to mark off all round the edge of the cake to give 6 equal sections. Join these marks with straight lines and cut the cake downwards completely straight along the lines to make the hexagonal shape.

A two-tier Hexagonal Wedding Cake is included in this book on pages 60-1.

To Make an Octagonal-Shaped Cake

An eight-sided cake may be cut quite simply from a square cake. Bake a square cake slightly larger than required, then carefully cut off each corner as evenly as possible to give eight sides all the same length.

All types of shaped cake tins are usually available to buy or hire from specialist cake decorating shops (see page 144) and some larger kitchen equipment stores.

Using a paper pattern as a guide to cutting a horseshoe-shaped cake

The final horseshoe-shaped cake and the pieces cut from the original round cake

Making the initial folds on a square piece of paper for a greaseproof paper icing bag

The icing bag completed, with the long edge taped into place

Making and Using a Greaseproof Paper Icing Bag

Almost all the piped decoration on the cakes in this book was done with home-made greaseproof paper icing bags, the usual tool of the professional. They are simple to make and it is a good idea to make up several at the same time.

1. Cut a piece of good-quality greaseproof paper to a square from 25-30 cm (10-12 inches). Fold in half to form a triangle.

2. Fold the triangle in half again to make a smaller triangle and press the folds firmly.

3. Open out and fold the bottom half of the triangle up to the folded line, creasing firmly.

4. Continue to fold the bag over and over again, creasing each fold firmly until it is complete. You should now have a cone shape.

5. Secure the join with clear sticky tape or fold the top point over twice to secure it. Cut off just sufficient from the tip to allow the chosen nozzle to fit neatly into the bag but so that only about one-third of the nozzle is showing.

6. Fill the bag not more than half full with icing. Fold over the top of the bag to keep the icing in the correct place, then push the icing down, so it is right in the nozzle. It is now ready to start.

It is easiest to use a paper icing bag for decorations, particularly when using royal and glacé icing, and it is equally good for butter creams. It is easier to manipulate than a nylon piping bag (which is much bigger and best kept for piping whipped cream on to cakes) or an icing pump (which tends to be cumbersome).

Icing nozzles

These are also known as tubes and pipes. There is a large variety of makes on the market which mainly fall into two types: the plain-based ones and the screw-on types, which need a connector when used with a plastic or nylon icing bag (but not with paper icing bags). Nozzles are sold by number, but this can be rather confusing as not all manufacturers use the same system. However, the plain writing nozzles are uniformly numbered, increasing in size from 00 to 0, 1, 2, 3, 4, although you will need to take care when choosing the larger ones as these do vary a little in size. To avoid confusion with the star nozzles, we have stipulated fine, medium or large instead of using numbers.

When buying nozzles do check that the seams are well joined and the shape of the hole even, otherwise your piped shape will always be uneven. Buy a good make, rather than the cheapest; which can be made of a softer metal which dents more easily. Always clean them properly after use and dry thoroughly before putting away to prevent rust.

Larger, or 'vegetable', nozzles are available for piping meringues and many of the butter cream designs, which need a heavy decoration. They are available in metal and plastic and come in a variety of shapes and sizes in plain and star. They are usually fitted into nylon or plastic icing bags rather than paper bags, although the paper icing bags can be made large enough to hold them. There is no need for a connector of any type with these nozzles.

Having selected your nozzles, decide what type of icing bag you will have. Paper icing bags made from greaseproof paper (see left) are the easiest to hold and manipulate but there are also nylon or plastic ones available. These also need a special connector to hold the nozzle. Some of these types require the screw-on nozzles, whilst others need the plain-based ones, which fit into the screw-on connector. They are not interchangeable; but you can use either type of nozzle with paper icing bags. Icing pumps are also available and can be used for simple decoration but they are extremely cumbersome and not practical for the delicate royal icing designs. If you have always used a pump, try the icing bag; with practice you will soon manipulate it with ease.

Icing techniques

These techniques can be seen in use on cakes throughout chapters 2 and 3.

Straight lines Place the tip of the nozzle where the line is to begin, press the icing and as it emerges, lift the nozzle about 2.5 cm (1 inch) above the surface. Move the hand in the direction you want to take the line and the icing will follow but use the other hand to steady the bag and keep the icing emerging evenly or the line will become uneven or break. Just before where the line should end, lower the tip of the nozzle back to the surface and break it off evenly with a quick movement. By keeping the icing above the surface, even shaky hands can achieve straight lines, for the icing can be moved back and forth until it is straight. If you finish with a blob of icing or the icing breaks, it can be lifted off with a skewer or cocktail stick. When piping another line either on top of or across the previous one, wait until the under line of icing is completely dry, otherwise if a mistake is made and you attempt to lift the wet icing, all the others will come away too.

Lattice work (see page 47). This must be done with completely straight lines, as wobbling will ruin the effect.

Dots Hold the nozzle upright with the tip just touching the surface. Squeeze the bag gently to allow the icing to emerge and at the same time lift the nozzle. Continue squeezing until the size of dot you require is achieved. Remove the nozzle quickly with a slight down and up movement. Lift any tail off with a cocktail stick.

Lacework Hold the nozzle almost upright and just above the surface, so that the icing flows easily. Work with a movement like scribbling and keep the nozzle moving around quickly and easily to form the pattern. Very fine, fine or medium nozzles are used.

Writing For accurate or block lettering, first prick out the design on to the cake, then follow using a writing nozzle. For a freehand pattern it is still wise to write on a piece of paper first to see how much space the words take up. Always allow the first layer to dry completely before adding the next and use the same colour as the base icing of the cake. For overpiping, any colour can be used but again leave the under icing to dry otherwise the colour is likely to run.

Curved lines Draw lines on paper and practise on these before actually piping on to the cake. Always prick out a curved line and if it is for the sides of the cake, it may be necessary to get someone else to hold the cake carefully on its side or at least tilted.

Stars Place a star nozzle in the bag and hold it upright and just above the surface. Pipe out the size of the star required, then quickly lift off with a down and up movement just as for the dots. They should be kept fairly flat not pulled up to a point in the centre.

Rosettes or Whirls These are piped in a similar way to stars but in a circular movement. Begin just above the surface and move the nozzle in a complete circle to enclose the middle. Finish off quickly to leave a slightly raised point in the centre. They can be varied by the type and size of star nozzle used.

Shells Use a star or special shell nozzle. Hold the icing bag and nozzle at an angle to the surface and a little above it. Start in the centre of the shell and first move the nozzle away from you, keeping an even pressure of icing, then back towards you with a little more pressure for the 'fat' part of the shell. Release the pressure and allow the icing to tail off and pull off sharply to make a point. Begin the next one over the point to hide it.

Scrolls These need a little practice to make perfect. Use a star or shell nozzle and hold the icing bag as for a straight line. Keep the nozzle just above the surface. For a question mark shape, begin with a fairly thick head and gradually release the pressure while finishing off in a long pointed tail. For a twisted scroll, twist the nozzle in a clockwise action. By varying the pressure on the icing bag you can also graduate the size of the scroll.

Icing nozzles, from the top: small, medium and large star nozzles; small shell, large shell and ribbon nozzles

Templates

Very soon after you become interested in decorating cakes, you will want to put patterns or designs on top of the cakes. For this it is necessary to have a guide or template, which is placed on top of the base-iced cake to help achieve an exactly symmetrical design. A template can only be used on a hard icing, such as royal icing or fondant moulding paste, as softer icings are marked by the templates.

It is also possible to buy metal or plastic symmetrical rings and cake markers, which help to make curves and scroll shapes on cakes.

Templates are first drawn on thick paper or thin card with the help of rulers, compasses or anything else which will assist in drawing the design or shape you require. Begin with a square or a circle the same size or about 2.5 cm (1 inch) smaller in width than the cake, depending on the size of the cake. The template must be exact and symmetrical in all ways, because if it is only a little irregular, the whole design of the cake will be spoilt. Once you have made the template it can be kept and used repeatedly. For ease of movement from the cake it is wise to cut a 'V' in the centre, which can be bent up rather like a handle.

The template should be positioned centrally on the cake. If it is being used for an outline, you then pipe just round the outside using a piping bag and writing nozzle. If it is for some other type of piping, then the design must be pricked out so it remains on top of the cake; simply use a long sharp pin and prick straight through the card or paper to the icing, so that a design is left clearly visible.

A template can also be made for the sides of the cake and is essential if curves or scallops are incorporated into the design.

Don't forget that with tiered cakes you need to make similar templates in graduated sizes to fit each tier.

When piping out the design keep as close as possible to the template, or pipe absolutely over the pin-pricked design keeping the curves even. Where sharp corners are required, break the icing at the corner and start again. Trim off with a pin if the icing is not absolutely even. Do not lift off the template until the piped outline is completely dry, otherwise you are likely to disturb the piping.

Other designs can be worked freehand, but if it is to be even in any way, then a template is a necessity.

To Make a Template for a Round Cake

1. Cut a circle of paper the size of the top of the cake or up to 2.5 cm (1 inch) smaller.
2. For an 8-point design, fold the circle in half then into quarters and again into eighths, creasing the folds firmly.
3. For a 6-point design, fold the circle first in half then carefully into 3 making sure each piece is exactly even (it is most accurate if you use a compass).
4. Check the design and how it needs to be drawn on to the folded paper, then draw it. Cut out carefully and open out the template, to check whether it is correct. If preferred, the template can be drawn on greaseproof paper first to make sure it is right, before transferring to thick paper or card.

To Make a Template for a Square Cake

1. Cut a square of greaseproof or other paper the size of the top of the cake or up to 2.5 cm (1 inch) smaller.
2. For a 4-point design, fold the square in half diagonally to give a triangle, then in half again to give a smaller triangle.
3. For an 8-point design, fold in half a third time to give a still-smaller triangle.

To Make a Template for the Sides of a Cake

1. For a round cake, measure the circumference of the cake with a piece of string, then use to cut a strip of paper the length of the sides and the depth of

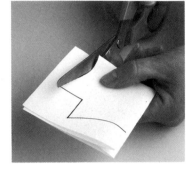

Cutting a template for a cake from marked thick paper or thin card

Pricking out a pattern on an iced cake, using the template as a guide

the cake. If a 4- or 8-point design, fold the paper into quarters or eighths, then draw the design on to the section, and cut right through the rest to give a design to reach around the whole cake. If a 6-point design, fold into sixths and cut as before. If preferred, the shape can be transferred to thick paper (but not card), so that it is firm enough to be held around the sides of the cake whilst the design is pricked out or is outlined in icing. If it is a difficult pattern to follow, for instance with lots of curves, it is simpler if the cake is tilted while you ice.

2. For a square cake, it is necessary only to cut a piece of paper the size of one side of the cake (provided they are all symmetrical). Halve this and draw the design, then cut out, unfold and use as for a round cake, holding the template against each side in turn.

Folding and cutting diagram for templates for cakes from chapters 2 and 3; dark grey areas indicate the shape of the fully folded template before cutting.

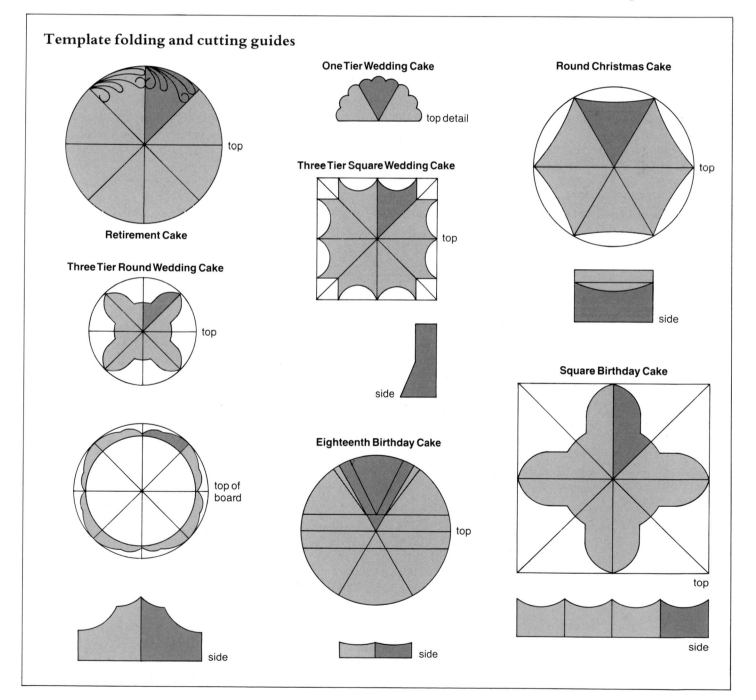

Template folding and cutting guides

Retirement Cake — top

Three Tier Round Wedding Cake — top

top of board

side

One Tier Wedding Cake — top detail

Three Tier Square Wedding Cake — top

side

Eighteenth Birthday Cake — top

side

Round Christmas Cake — top

side

Square Birthday Cake — top

side

The Basic Recipes

Ideally, all cakes and icings should be made by hand and, of course, not that long ago there was little or no electrical equipment available to help. Today, extra help, particularly with the physical hard work of beating, is welcome and cakes can be made with an electric mixer with good results. Most of the icings can, too, but with varying results.

Large mixers, whether free-standing or hand-held, make creaming and whisking comparatively easy. Large fruit cakes are best made in a large mixer, as the quantity needed to be creamed may cause a smaller mixer to overheat.

Butter cream and some icings are good made with a mixer, but with royal icing the extra speed of beating incorporates too many air bubbles which are very difficult to disperse. A hand-held mixer is better than a large one and may be used for just the first part of the mixing. When completed, royal icing made in a mixer should be put into an airtight polythene or plastic container, covered and banged hard on the floor several times to help bring the air bubbles to the surface and burst. Leave it to stand for at least 6 hours and preferably overnight before using. This allows bubbles to disperse. Before using, mix well but not too vigorously or you will reintroduce more air.

Food processors are ideal for some parts of cake and icing preparation such as chopping and grating, but many are not recommended for whisking.

The microwave cooker is good for melting chocolate, softening butter prior to creaming, and melting ingredients for some of the icings.

With a conventional oven it is worthwhile checking that the temperature is accurate if you are making a lot of cakes. On the whole, manufacturers set ovens slightly lower than the temperature stated, for obvious reasons, but should you find things tend to over-brown or cook more quickly than stated, it is a good idea to test the temperature with a simple oven thermometer. If this shows you have a problem, call in the appropriate service to test and adjust the oven.

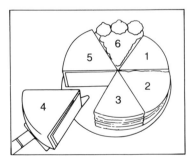

1. Madeira Cake
2. Whisked Sponge filled with crème pâtissière and iced with Fudge Frosting
3. Quick Mix Sponge filled with butter cream
4. Rich Fruit Cake with Sherry with marzipan and royal icing
5. Light Fruit Cake with a layer of marzipan
6. Meringue Cuite

LIGHT FRUIT CAKE

This is a moist well-flavoured cake which has grated apple in it to help with the moisture, but it does not keep for longer than about 2 weeks. It is therefore better to use it only for a simply decorated cake. It can be covered with marzipan as with all fruit cakes and with any of the icings.

The currants suggested in the recipe may be replaced with finely chopped, stoned dates or with a mixture of finely chopped, no-need-to-soak dried apricots and stoned, chopped prunes.

Preparation time: about 20 minutes
Cooking time: see chart
Oven: 180°C, 350°F, Gas Mark 4

1. Grease and double-line the chosen tin (page 8).
2. Sift the flour, bicarbonate of soda, spice and ginger into a bowl.
3. In another bowl cream the butter or margarine with the sifted brown sugar until very light, fluffy and pale in colour.
4. Beat in the eggs one at a time, following each with a spoonful of the flour mixture, then fold in the remaining flour.

5. Mix the raisins, currants, sultanas, peel and fruit rind together and add to the mixture.
6. Peel, core and coarsely grate the apples, add to the mixture and stir through evenly.
7. Turn the mixture into the prepared tin, level the top and bake for the time suggested on the chart, in the centre of the oven. The largest size of cake is better if the oven is turned down to 160°C, 325°F, Gas Mark 3 after 1½ hours to prevent over-browning.
8. To test if the cake is done, insert a skewer into the centre, it should come out clean, then cool in the tin for 5 minutes. Turn out on to a wire tray and leave until cold. When cold wrap in foil or put into an air-tight container for 24–48 hours before use.

This fruit cake will keep well in the freezer for up to 3 months. Do not remove the lining paper from around the cake once it has cooled, but wrap it straight from the tin securely in foil.

Opposite: square and round versions of the Light Fruit Cake

LIGHT FRUIT CAKE INGREDIENTS				
CAKE SIZES	18 cm (7 in) round 15 cm (6 in) square	20 cm (8 in) round 18 cm (7 in) square	23 cm (9 in) round 20 cm (8 in) square	25 cm (10 in) round 23 cm (9 in) square
plain flour	175 g (6 oz)	225 g (8 oz)	350 g (12 oz)	450 g (1 lb)
bicarbonate of soda	⅓ teaspoon	½ teaspoon	¾ teaspoon	1 teaspoon
mixed spice	⅓ teaspoon	½ teaspoon	¾ teaspoon	1 teaspoon
ground ginger	good pinch	¼ teaspoon	⅓ teaspoon	½ teaspoon
butter or margarine	100 g (4 oz)	175 g (6 oz)	250 g (9 oz)	350 g (12 oz)
light soft brown sugar	100 g (4 oz)	175 g (6 oz)	250 g (9 oz)	350 g (12 oz)
eggs	2 (size 3 or 4)	2 (size 1 or 2)	3 (size 1 or 2)	4 (size 1 or 2)
raisins	175 g (6 oz)	225 g (8 oz)	350 g (12 oz)	450 g (1 lb)
currants	75 g (3 oz)	100 g (4 oz)	175 g (6 oz)	225 g (8 oz)
sultanas	75 g (3 oz)	100 g (4 oz)	175 g (6 oz)	225 g (8 oz)
cut mixed peel	40 g (1½ oz)	50 g (2 oz)	75 g (3 oz)	100 g (4 oz)
grated orange or lemon rind	1	1	1½-2	2
cooking apple	100 g (4 oz)	175 g (6 oz)	250 g (9 oz)	350 g (12 oz)
approx cooking time	1-1¼ hours	1¼-1½ hours	about 1¾ hours	2-2¼ hours

RICH FRUIT CAKE

Preparation time: about 30 minutes
Cooking time: see chart
Oven: 150°C, 300°F, Gas
                      Mark 2

This fruit cake improves with keeping and makes a delicious Christmas cake. For the smaller cakes, especially the top tiers of a wedding cake, it is often a good idea to add a little gravy browning (about 1 teaspoon) to the mixture, so that it will be the same colour as the larger cakes which tend to go darker with the length of cooking necessary.

1. Grease and double-line the cake tin (page 8).
2. Mix together the currants, sultanas and raisins in a large bowl.
3. Cut the glacé cherries into quarters, rinse under warm water, dry

Rich Fruit Cake with a double layer of lining paper

thoroughly on paper towels or a clean cloth.
4. Add the cherries to the dried fruit mixture with the mixed peel, almonds and grated lemon rind. Mix well.
5. Sift the flour, ground cinnamon and mixed spice together.
6. Cream the butter until soft, then add the sugar and continue creaming until light, fluffy and much paler in colour. Do not overbeat or the cake will become coarse in texture and heavy.
7. Add the eggs to the creamed mixture one at a time, beating in thoroughly and following each with a spoonful of flour.
8. Fold in the remaining flour, followed by the dried fruit mixture.
9. Add the black treacle, if liked.
10. Turn into the prepared tin and level the top. Using the back of a spoon, make a slight hollow in the centre of the mixture, so that the top of the cake comes out flat when baked.
11. Fold sheets of brown paper into long narrow strips of about 6 thicknesses and tie around the outside of the tin for protection during cooking. Place in a preheated oven and bake for the time suggested in the chart. If the cake seems to be overbrowning, lay a sheet of greaseproof paper lightly over the top. With very large cakes it is sometimes better to turn the oven down to 140°C, 275°F, Gas Mark 1 after about three-quarters of the cooking time has been completed.
12. To test if the cake is done, insert a skewer in the centre: it should come out clean. Remove from the oven and leave to cool in the tin. Turn on to a wire tray and remove the lining paper.
13. Prick the top of the cake all over with a skewer, then spoon several tablespoons of brandy or other spirit over the top. Wrap in greaseproof paper and foil and store. If possible repeat this process at 2 weekly intervals while maturing. This cake should be allowed to mature for 2-3 months but can be used perfectly well after 2 weeks or so. It will keep for 6-8 months.

RICH FRUIT CAKE INGREDIENTS

SQUARE	13 cm (5 inch)	15 cm (6 inch)	18 cm (7 inch)	20 cm (8 inch)	23 cm (9 inch)	25 cm (10 inch)	28 cm (11 inch)	30 cm (12 inch)
ROUND or PETAL SHAPED	15 cm (6 inch)	18 cm (7 inch)	20 cm (8 inch)	23 cm (9 inch)	25 cm (10 inch)	28 cm (11 inch)	30 cm (12 inch)	
SLAB CAKE				29×21×4 cm (11½×8½×1½ inch)	30×25×5 cm (12×10×2 inch)			
currants	150 g (5 oz)	225 g (8 oz)	350 g (12 oz)	450 g (1 lb)	625 g (1lb 6 oz)	775 g (1lb 12 oz)	1.2 kg (2lb 8 oz)	1.4 kg (3 lb)
sultanas	50 g (2 oz)	90 g (3½ oz)	125 g (4½ oz)	200 g (7 oz)	225 g (8 oz)	375 g (13 oz)	400 g (14 oz)	500 g (1lb 2 oz)
raisins	50 g (2 oz)	90 g (3½ oz)	125 g (4½ oz)	200 g (7 oz)	225 g (8 oz)	375 g (13 oz)	400 g (14 oz)	500 g (1lb 2 oz)
glacé cherries	40 g (1½ oz)	65 g (2½ oz)	75 g (3 oz)	100 g (4 oz)	150 g (5 oz)	225 g (8 oz)	300 g (10 oz)	350 g (12 oz)
mixed peel, chopped	25 g (1 oz)	50 g (2 oz)	50 g (2 oz)	75 g (3 oz)	100 g (4 oz)	150 g (5 oz)	200 g (7 oz)	250 g (9 oz)
blanched almonds, chopped	25 g (1 oz)	50 g (2 oz)	50 g (2 oz)	75 g (3 oz)	100 g (4 oz)	150 g (5 oz)	200 g (7 oz)	250 g (9 oz)
lemon rind, grated	¼ lemon	½ lemon	¾ lemon	1 lemon	1 lemon	1 lemon	1½ lemons	2 lemons
plain flour	100 g (3½ oz)	175 g (6 oz)	200 g (7½ oz)	350 g (12 oz)	400 g (14 oz)	600 g (1lb 5 oz)	700 g (1lb 8 oz)	825 g (1lb 13 oz)
ground cinnamon	½ teaspoon	½ teaspoon	¾ teaspoon	1 teaspoon	1½ teaspoons	2 teaspoons	2½ teaspoons	2¾ teaspoons
ground mixed spice	¼ teaspoon	¼ teaspoon	½ teaspoon	¾ teaspoon	1 teaspoon	1¼ teaspoons	1½ teaspoons	1¾ teaspoons
butter	75 g (3 oz)	150 g (5 oz)	175 g (6 oz)	275 g (10 oz)	350 g (12 oz)	500 g (1lb 2 oz)	600 g (1lb 5 oz)	800 g (1lb 12 oz)
soft brown sugar	75 g (3 oz)	150 g (5 oz)	175 g (6 oz)	275 g (10 oz)	350 g (12 oz)	500 g (1lb 2 oz)	600 g (1lb 5 oz)	800 g (1lb 12 oz)
eggs (size 2)	1½	2½	3	5	6	9	11	14
black treacle (optional)	1 teaspoon	1 teaspoon	1 tablespoon	1 tablespoon	1 tablespoon	2 tablespoons	2 tablespoons	2 tablespoons
approx cooking time	*2 hours*	*2½ hours*	*2¾ hours*	*3¼ hours*	*3¾ hours*	*4¼-4½ hours*	*5¼-5½ hours*	*6-6½ hours*
approx cooked weight	*750 g (1½ lb)*	*1.25 kg (2½ lb)*	*1.5 kg (3¼ lb)*	*2 kg (4½ lb)*	*2.75 kg (6 lb)*	*4 kg (9 lb)*	*5 kg (11 lb)*	*6.5 kg (14 lb)*
brandy, added after cooking	2 tablespoons	3 tablespoons	3 tablespoons	4 tablespoons	5 tablespoons	6 tablespoons	7 tablespoons	8 tablespoons

RICH FRUIT CAKE WITH SHERRY

This is a recipe of graduated sizes for a special occasion. It has fewer currants and more cherries than many recipes and is baked with sherry in it. It should be left to mature for 2-4 weeks before use and will keep for much longer if 'doctored' with sherry or brandy poured over the surface every 2 weeks for up to 2 months. It can also be made into a rich Dundee by covering the top of the unbaked cake with blanched whole almonds; or turned into a spectacular fruit cake by adding glacé fruits and nuts to the top of the baked cake with a coating of warmed and sieved apricot jam.

Preparation time: 30-40 minutes
Cooking time: see chart
Oven: 150°C, 300°F, Gas Mark 2

Rich Fruit Cake with Sherry showing the even spread of the fruit in a well baked cake

1. Grease and double-line the cake tin (page 8).
2. Weigh out the dried fruits – currants, sultanas, raisins and peel – and put into a large bowl. Add the ground almonds.
3. Quarter the cherries, wash off all the sticky syrup, drain and dry thoroughly on paper towels on a clean cloth. Add to the fruit with the grated rinds of the lemon and orange.
4. Cream the butter and sugar together until light, fluffy and pale in colour.
5. Measure out the sherry. Add the treacle and gravy browning to the creamed mixture, beating in until completely incorporated.
6. Weigh out the flours and sift into another bowl with the spices.

RICH FRUIT CAKE WITH SHERRY INGREDIENT	
ROUND TIN:	13 cm (5 inch)
depth:	5 cm (2 inch)
weight:	625 g (1 lb 6 oz)
cooking time:	2¼ hours
SHALLOW SQUARE:	13 cm (5 inch)
depth:	4.75 cm (1⅞ inch)
weight:	625 g (1 lb 6 oz)
cooking time:	2¼ hours
DEEP SQUARE:	
depth:	
weight:	
cooking time:	
currants	100 g (4 oz)
sultanas	100 g (4 oz)
raisins	50 g (2 oz)
mixed peel	40 g (1½ oz)
ground almonds	15 g (½ oz)
glacé cherries	50 g (2 oz)
lemon rind	½ lemon
orange rind	½ orange
butter	65 g (2½ oz)
dark soft brown sugar	65 g (2½ oz)
eggs (size 1 or 2)	1
sherry	2 teaspoons
black treacle	1 teaspoon
gravy browning	½ teaspoon
self-raising flour	25 g (1 oz)
plain flour	50 g (2 oz)
ground cinnamon	¼ teaspoon
mixed spice	good pinch
ground nutmeg	pinch

7. Beat the eggs into the creamed mixture, one at a time, following each with 2 tablespoons of the flour. Fold in the rest of the flour alternating with the sherry.

8. Mix in the dried fruit mixture evenly and turn in to the prepared tin. Make sure there is sufficient mixture in the corners of the tin, and level the top.

9. Fold sheets of brown paper into narrow strips of about 6 thicknesses and tie round the outside of the cake tin for protection during cooking.

10. Cook in the preheated oven following the times suggested in the chart. Large rich cakes should be placed towards the bottom of the oven or at least below the centre. Ovens do vary in temperature, so it is wise to test the cake 15 minutes before the stated time (equally they may need an extra 15 minutes or so if the oven is on the cool side). To test, insert a metal skewer in the centre of the cake – it should come out clean. If at all sticky, return to the oven for 15 minutes and test again.

11. Remove the cake from the oven when ready and leave to cool in the tin. Turn out, do not remove the wrapping paper but wrap the whole thing in foil and leave for at least 2 weeks before use. If keeping the cake, prick the top all over with a skewer and spoon 2-8 tablespoons brandy or sherry over the surface (depending on the size of the cake) before wrapping. This process may be repeated at 2 weekly intervals for up to 2 months.

15 cm (6 inch)	18 cm (7 inch)	20 cm (8 inch)	23 cm (9 inch)	25 cm (10 inch)	28 cm (11 inch)	30 cm (12 inch)
5.5 cm (2¼ inch)	6 cm (2½ inch)	6 cm (2½ inch)	6 cm (2½ inch)	7 cm (2¾ inch)	7 cm (2¾ inch)	7.5 cm (3 inch)
900 g (2 lb)	1.5 kg (3 lb)	1.75 kg (3¾ lb)	2.5 kg (5½ lb)	3.2 kg (7 lb 5 oz)	3.8 kg (8 lb 12 oz)	4.7 kg (10 lb 6 oz)
2¾ hours	3 hours	3½ hours	4 hours	4¼ hours	5 hours	5¾ hours
15 cm (6 inch)	18 cm (7 inch)	20 cm (8 inch)	23 cm (9 inch)	25 cm (10 inch)	28 cm (11 inch)	30 cm (12 inch)
5 cm (2 inch)	5.5 cm (2¼ inch)	5.5 cm (2¼ inch)	5.5 cm (2¼ inch)	5.6 cm (2⅓ inch)	5.6 cm (2⅓ inch)	6 cm (2½ inch)
900 g (2 lb)	1.5 kg (3 lb)	1.75 kg (3¾ lb)	2.5 kg (5½ lb)	3.2 kg (7 lb 5 oz)	3.8 kg (8 lb 12 oz)	4.7 kg (10 lb 6 oz)
2¼ hours	2¾ hours	3¼ hours	3¾ hours	4½ hours	4½ hours	5 hours
13 cm (5 inch)	15 cm (6 inch)	18 cm (7 inch)	20 cm (8 inch)	23 cm (9 inch)	25 cm (10 inch)	28 cm (11 inch)
7 cm (2¾ inch)	7 cm (2¾ inch)	7 cm (2¾ inch)	7.5 cm (3 inch)	7.5 cm (3 inch)	7.5 cm (3 inch)	7.5 cm (3 inch)
900 g (2 lb)	1.5 kg (3 lb)	1.75 kg (3¾ lb)	2.5 kg (5½ lb)	3.2 kg (7 lb 5 oz)	3.8 kg (8 lb 12 oz)	4.6 kg (10 lb 6 oz)
2½ hours	3 hours	3½ hours	4¼ hours	5 hours	5½ hours	5½ hours
165 g (5½ oz)	215 g (7½ oz)	300 g (11 oz)	450 g (1 lb)	625 g (1 lb 6 oz)	725 g (1 lb 10 oz)	950 g (1 lb 4 oz)
165 g (5½ oz)	215 g (7½ oz)	300 g (11 oz)	450 g (1 lb)	625 g (1 lb 6 oz)	725 g (1 lb 10 oz)	950 g (1 lb 14 oz)
75 g (3 oz)	150 g (5 oz)	200 g (7 oz)	275 g (10 oz)	350 g (12 oz)	400 g (14 oz)	450 g (1 lb)
50 g (2 oz)	65 g (2½ oz)	75 g (3 oz)	100 g (4 oz)	175 g (6 oz)	225 g (8 oz)	250 g (9 oz)
25 g (1 oz)	40 g (1½ oz)	50 g (2 oz)	75 g (3 oz)	100 g (4 oz)	150 g (5 oz)	175 g (6 oz)
75 g (3 oz)	90 g (3½ oz)	100 g (4 oz)	175 g (6 oz)	225 g (8 oz)	275 g (10 oz)	300 g (11 oz)
½ lemon	1 lemon	1 lemon	1½ lemons	2 lemons	2 lemons	2 lemons
½ orange	½ orange	½ orange	1 orange	1 orange	1 orange	1 orange
90 g (3½ oz)	150 g (5 oz)	200 g (7 oz)	275 g (10 oz)	400 g (14 oz)	475 g (1 lb 1 oz)	550 g (1 lb 4 oz)
90 g (3½ oz)	150 g (5 oz)	200 g (7 oz)	275 g (10 oz)	400 g (14 oz)	475 g (1 lb 1 oz)	550 g (1 lb 4 oz)
2	3	4	5	6	7	9
1 tablespoon	2 tablespoons	3 tablespoons	4 tablespoons	4½ tablespoons	5 tablespoons	6 tablespoons
1 teaspoon	2 teaspoons	1 tablespoon	1½ tablespoons	2 tablespoons	2½ tablespoons	3 tablespoons
½ teaspoon	1 teaspoon	1 teaspoon	1½ teaspoons	1½ teaspoons	1 teaspoon	1 teaspoon
40 g (1½ oz)	65 g (2½ oz)	65 g (2½ oz)	75 g (3 oz)	100 g (4 oz)	150 g (5 oz)	175 g (6 oz)
90 g (3½ oz)	120 g (4½ oz)	175 g (6 oz)	225 g (8 oz)	375 g (13 oz)	425 g (15 oz)	500 g (1 lb 2 oz)
¼ teaspoon	½ teaspoon	¾ teaspoon	1 teaspoon	1½ teaspoons	2 teaspoons	2¼ teaspoons
⅛ teaspoon	¼ teaspoon	½ teaspoon	¾ teaspoon	1¼ teaspoons	1½ teaspoons	1¾ teaspoons
good pinch	good pinch	good pinch	¼ teaspoon	½ teaspoon	¾ teaspoons	1 teaspoon

QUICK MIX CAKE

This is a very quick and easy cake to prepare and bake to use for many occasions. However, as it is made without proper creaming, its keeping qualities are not so good as a Victoria sandwich cake or Madeira, so should be baked, iced and used within a week for the best results. Consequently it is not advisable to use this cake for an elaborately iced and decorated cake using royal icing for a special occasion. In this instance, for non-fruit cake eaters, a Madeira cake should be used, as it has a much longer keeping life.

The quick mix cake can be baked in a variety of shapes and sizes and if you want to bake in something a different shape from those in the chart, simply fill your chosen baking container with water and see which size of tin from the chart holds the same amount of liquid – this will tell you the amount of mixture you will require. The baking may have to be watched a little carefully; if the container is shallower allow a little less time and if it is deeper allow a little longer before testing. Remember always to use a good quality soft tub margarine for this cake and don't forget to use baking powder.

Opposite: small cakes made from the Quick Mix Cake mixture and a cake mixed ready for baking

Preparation time: about 5 minutes
Cooking time: see chart
Oven: 160°C, 325°F, Gas Mark 3

1. Put the margarine, sugar, eggs, sifted flour and baking powder and vanilla essence into a bowl.
2. Mix together with a wooden spoon or hand-held electric mixer, then beat hard for 1-2 minutes until smooth and glossy.
3. Turn into a greased and floured (or single-lined and greased) tin and level the top. Bake in a preheated oven for the time suggested in the chart or until well risen, just firm to the touch and the sides of the cake are just beginning to shrink from the sides of the tin.
4. Cool for about 30 seconds in the tin, then loosen the sides of the cake from the tin and turn on to a wire tray. Invert the cake on to another wire tray, unless baked in a ring mould or basin. This prevents ugly marks from the wire tray which can show through a thin icing. Leave to cool.
5. The cake is now ready to fill and/or ice.

Variations:
Chocolate Quick Mix Cake – omit the vanilla essence and add 1 tablespoon sifted cocoa powder for the 2-egg mixture; 1½ tablespoons for the 3-egg mixture; 2 tablespoons for the 4-egg mixture; and 2½ tablespoons for the 5-egg mixture.

Coffee Quick Mix Cake – omit the vanilla essence and add 2 teaspoons instant coffee powder (not granules) or 1 tablespoon coffee essence for the 2-

QUICK MIX CAKE INGREDIENTS

CAKE SIZES	2×18 cm (7 inch) sandwich tins	18 paper cake cases or patty tins	20 cm (8 inch) sandwich tin 20 cm (8 inch) ring mould 18 cm (7 inch) deep square tin	900ml (1½ pint) pudding basin*	about 26 paper cake cases or patty tins	2×20 cm (8 inch) sandwich tins
soft (tub) margarine, chilled	100 g (4 oz)	100 g (4 oz)	100 g (4 oz)	100 g (4 oz)	175 g (6 oz)	175 g (6 oz)
caster sugar	100 g (4 oz)	100 g (4 oz)	100 g (4 oz)	100 g (4 oz)	175 g (6 oz)	175 g (6 oz)
eggs (size 1 or 2)	2	2	2	2	3	3
self-raising flour	100 g (4 oz)	100 g (4 oz)	100 g (4 oz)	100 g (4 oz)	175 g (6 oz)	175 g (6 oz)
baking powder	1 teaspoon	1 teaspoon	1 teaspoon	1 teaspoon	1½ teaspoons	1½ teaspoons
vanilla essence	4 drops	4 drops	4 drops	4 drops	6 drops	6 drops
approx cooking time	25-30 minutes	15-20 minutes	35-40 minutes	about 50 minutes	15-20 minutes	30-35 minutes

* add 25 g (1 oz) cornflower sifted with the flour

egg mixture; 1 tablespoon coffee powder or 1½ tablespoons coffee essence for 3-egg mixture; 4 tablespoons coffee powder or 2 tablespoons coffee essence for the 4-egg mixture; and 5 teaspoons coffee powder or 2½ tablespoons coffee essence for the 5-egg mixture.

Orange or Lemon Quick Mix Cake – omit the vanilla essence and add 2 teaspoons finely grated orange or lemon rind for the 2-egg mixture; 3 teaspoons for the 3-egg mixture; 4 teaspoons for the 4-egg mixture; and 5 teaspoons for the 5-egg mixture.

Spiced Quick Mix Cake – add 1 teaspoon mixed spice, ground cinnamon or ground ginger for the 2-egg mixture; 1½ teaspoons for the 3-egg mixture; 2 teaspoons for the 4-egg mixture; and 2½ teaspoons for the 5 egg mixture.

Nut Quick Mix Cake – add 40 g (1½ oz) finely chopped or grated walnuts, hazelnuts, pecans, unsalted peanuts or toasted almonds to the 2-egg mixture; 50 g (2 oz) to the 3-egg mixture; 65 g (2½ oz) to the 4-egg mixture; and 75 g (3 oz) to the 5-egg mixture.

Fudgy Quick Mix Cake – replace from half to all the caster sugar with sifted light soft brown sugar for all the sizes of cake.

23 cm (9 inch) deep sandwich tin	2 oval oven-proof 600-700ml (1-1¼ pint) glass dishes	28×18×4 cm (11×7×1½ inch) slab cake 20 cm (8 inch) round or petal tin 20 cm (8 inch) square tin	1 litre (2 pint) pudding basin*	29×21×4 cm (11½×8½×1½ inch) slab cake	23 cm (9 inch) round or petal tin 23 cm (9 inch) square tin	30×25×5 cm (12×10×2 inch) slab cake
175 g (6 oz)	175 g (6 oz)	175 g (6 oz)	175 g (6 oz)	225 g (8 oz)	225 g (8 oz)	275 g (10 oz)
175 g (6 oz)	175 g (6 oz)	175 g (6 oz)	175 g (6 oz)	225 g (8 oz)	225 g (8 oz)	275 g (10 oz)
3	3	3	3	4	4	5
175 g (6 oz)	175 g (6 oz)	175 g (6 oz)	175 g (6 oz)	225 g (8 oz)	225 g (8 oz)	275 g (10 oz)
1½ teaspoons	1½ teaspoons	1½ teaspoons	1½ teaspoons	2 teaspoons	2 teaspoons	2½ teaspoons
6 drops	6 drops	6 drops	6 drops	8 drops	8 drops	10 drops
about 45 minutes	40-45 minutes	35-40 minutes	about 1 hour	about 40 minutes	about 1 hour	50-60 minutes

WHISKED SPONGE CAKE

The butter in this recipe is added for extra keeping quality but it can be omitted if preferred. Without the added fat the cake should be eaten within 48 hours, with fat it should keep for 48 hours longer, but it does not keep indefinitely in prime condition.

This cake will freeze for up to 2 months if wrapped securely in foil or put into a rigid container; take care as it can easily be damaged without good protection.

Preparation time: 10–15 minutes
Cooking time: see chart
Oven: see chart

1. Line the chosen tin with non-stick silicone paper or greased, greaseproof paper.
2. Put the eggs and sugar into a heatproof bowl over a saucepan of hot but not boiling water. Whisk until the mixture becomes very thick and pale in colour and the whisk leaves a heavy trail when lifted. Remove the bowl from the saucepan and continue whisking until the mixture is cool. Alternatively the whisking may be done with an electric mixer when no added heat is necessary.
3. Sift the flour and baking powder together, then sift again over the whisked mixture. Using a metal spoon, fold in the flour quickly and evenly, followed by the cooled but still runny butter (if used).
4. Turn into the prepared tin(s) and shake gently or spread out lightly with a palette knife until even, making sure there is plenty of mixture in the corners. Bake for the times suggested in the chart or until the cake springs back when gently pressed with the fingertips and has begun to shrink a little from the sides of the tin.
5. Turn on to a wire tray and remove the lining paper. Leave to cool.
6. If making a Swiss roll, invert the cake on to a sheet of greaseproof paper sprinkled liberally with caster sugar or on to a sheet of non-stick silicone paper without the sugar, unless specified. Quickly peel off the lining paper and trim the edges of the cake with a sharp knife. Fold the top short edge of the cake in about 2.5 cm (1 inch), then roll up the cake loosely with the paper inside. (This process must be done immediately the cake is taken out of the oven for it will not roll up without cracking if it is allowed to cool any more than necessary.) Fold back the top of the paper, so that it does not stick to the cake as it cools and spoil the top surface.
7. Leave to cool for a few minutes for the cake to set, then carefully unroll and remove the paper.
8. Fill with jam, butter cream or fruit and whipped cream, and roll up again.

Variations:
Lemon or Orange Whisked Sponge Cake: add the grated rind of ½ lemon or orange with the flour.
Chocolate Whisked Sponge Cake: replace 15 g (½ oz) flour with sifted cocoa powder.
Coffee Whisked Sponge Cake: add 2 teaspoons instant coffee powder (not granules) to the mixture with the flour.
Spiced Whisked Sponge Cake: add ½ teaspoon ground cinnamon, mixed spice or ground ginger sifted with the flour.
Walnut Whisked Sponge Cake: add 25–40 g (1–1½ oz) very finely chopped or ground walnuts, folded into the cake mixture with the butter.

Opposite: Swiss roll and round cakes made from the Whisked Sponge Cake recipe

WHISKED SPONGE CAKE INGREDIENTS	
CAKE SIZES	2×18 cm (7 inch) sandwich tins
eggs (size 1 or 2)	2
caster sugar	50 g (2 oz)
plain flour	50 g (2 oz)
baking powder	½ teaspoon
melted butter (optional)	15 g (½ oz)
approx cooking time	20–25 minutes
oven	180°C, 350°F, Gas Mark 4

20 cm (8in) sandwich tin 18 cm (7 inch) square tin	28×18 cm (11×7 inch) Swiss roll tin	18 sponge drops	20 cm (8 inch) round cake tin	2×20 cm (8 inch) sandwich tins	28×18×4 cm (11×7×1½ inch) slab cake	30×23 cm (12×9 inch) Swiss roll tin	30×23 cm (12×9 inch) Swiss roll tin
2	2	2	3	3	3	3	4
50 g (2 oz)	50 g (2 oz)	50 g (2 oz)	75 g (3 oz)	75 g (3 oz)	75 g (3 oz)	75 g (3 oz)	100 g (4 oz)
50 g (2 oz)	50 g (2 oz)	50 g (2 oz)	75 g (3 oz)	75 g (3 oz)	75 g (3 oz)	75 g (3 oz)	100 g (4 oz)
½ teaspoon	½ teaspoon	½ teaspoon	½ teaspoon	½ teaspoon	½ teaspoon	½ teaspoon	½ teaspoon
15 g (½ oz)	15 g (½ oz)	15 g (½ oz)	25 g (1 oz)	25 g (1 oz)	25 g (1 oz)	25 g (1 oz)	25 g (1 oz)
25–30 minutes	10–12 minutes	5–10 minutes	35–40 minutes	20–25 minutes	30–35 minutes	12–15 minutes	15–20 minutes
180°C, 350°F, Gas Mark 4	190°C, 375°F, Gas Mark 5	190°C, 375°F, Gas Mark 5	180°C, 350°F, Gas Mark 4	180°C, 350°F, Gas Mark 4	180°C, 350°F, Gas Mark 4	200°C, 400°F, Gas Mark 6	190°C, 375°F, Gas Mark 5

MADEIRA CAKE

Madeira cake can be covered with marzipan and royal or fondant moulding paste or other icing. It may also be brushed with apricot glaze and simply covered in fondant moulding paste. The traditional flavouring of lemon rind and juice may be replaced with orange for an Orange Madeira or altered as in the variations below.

Preparation time: about 15-20 minutes.
Cooking time: see chart
Oven: 160°C, 325°F, Gas Mark 3

1. Grease and single-line the chosen tin (page 8).
2. Cream the butter and sugar together until light, fluffy and very pale.
3. Sift the flours together. Beat in the eggs, one at a time, following each with a spoonful of the flours.
4. Fold the rest of the flours into the creamed mixture followed by the grated lemon rind and juice.
5. Turn into the prepared tin and level the top.
6. Bake in a preheated oven for the time suggested or until well risen, firm to the touch and golden brown.
7. Cool in the tin for 5-10 minutes, then turn out on to a wire tray and leave until cold. Do not peel off the lining paper but wrap as it is in foil or store in an airtight container until

MADEIRA CAKE INGREDIENTS

CAKE SIZES	15 cm (6 inch) round or square tin	18 cm (7 inch) round tin	18 cm (7 inch) round tin* 900 g (2lb) loaf tin	18 cm (7 inch) square tin	20 cm (8 inch) round or petal shaped tin	20 cm (8 inch) round or petal shaped tin*	20 cm (8 inch) square tin
butter	100 g (4 oz)	100 g (4 oz)	150 g (6 oz)	150 g (6 oz)	150 g (6 oz)	200 g (8 oz)	200 g (8 oz)
caster sugar	100 g (4 oz)	100 g (4 oz)	150 g (6 oz)	150 g (6 oz)	150 g (6 oz)	200 g (8 oz)	200 g (8 oz)
self-raising flour	100 g (4 oz)	100 g (4 oz)	150 g (6 oz)	150 g (6 oz)	150 g (6 oz)	200 g (8 oz)	200 g (8 oz)
plain flour	50 g (2 oz)	50 g (2 oz)	75 g (3 oz)	75 g (3 oz)	75 g (3 oz)	100 g (4 oz)	100 g (4 oz)
eggs	2	2	3	3	3	4	4
grated lemon rind	½-1 lemon	½-1 lemon	1 lemon	1 lemon	1 lemon	1½ lemons	1½ lemons
approx cooking time	1 hour	50 minutes	1¼ hours	1 hour and 5-10 minutes	1 hour	1 hour and 15-20 minutes	1 hour and 15-20 minutes

* These quantities make a deeper cake

required. If to be iced, leave for at least 24 hours to allow the cake to settle. Madeira cakes may be frozen for up to 6 months. Thaw out still in the wrapping at room temperature.

Variations:
Ginger: omit the lemon rind and add 1 teaspoon ground ginger to the 2-egg mixture plus 2 pieces finely chopped stem ginger, if liked. Add 1½ teaspoons ground ginger to the 3-egg mixture; and 2 teaspoons to the 4-egg mixture with more chopped stem ginger as desired.
Coffee Walnut: omit the lemon rind and replace the lemon juice with coffee essence. Add 40 g (1½ oz) finely chopped walnuts to the 2-egg mixture; 50 g (2 oz) walnuts to the 3-egg mixture; and 65 g (2½ oz) walnuts to the 4-egg mixture.

VICTORIA SANDWICH CAKE

150 g (6 oz) caster sugar
150 g (6 oz) butter or soft margarine
3 eggs (size 1 or 2)
150 g (6 oz) self-raising flour
1 tablespoon cold water
few drops of vanilla essence

Preparation time: about 30 minutes
Cooking time: 20-25 minutes
Oven: 190°C, 375°F, Gas Mark 5

1. Grease two 20 cm (8 inch) round sandwich tins and either dust with flour or bottom line with greaseproof paper and grease again. Alternatively grease and flour or bottom line a rectangular tin 28 × 18 × 4 cm (11 × 7 × 1½ inch).
2. Cream the sugar and butter or margarine together until light, fluffy and very pale in colour.
3. Beat in the eggs, one at a time following each with a spoonful of the flour.
4. Sift the remaining flour and fold into the mixture alternating with the water. Finally add the essence.
5. Divide between the cake tins, or fill the larger tin and level the tops. Bake in a preheated oven for 20-25 minutes or until well risen and firm to the touch. The larger cake may take a few minutes longer. Turn out on to a wire tray and leave to cool.

Variations:
Chocolate: replace 25 g (1 oz) of the flour with sifted cocoa powder and add ½ level teaspoon baking powder with the flour.
Coffee: replace the water with coffee essence or dissolve 2 teaspoons instant coffee in 1 tablespoon boiling water, cool and use in place of the water.
Lemon or Orange: omit the vanilla essence and add the very finely grated rind of 1 lemon or 1 orange. The water may be replaced with fruit juice.
Fudge: replace the caster sugar with sifted light soft brown sugar.

Alternate sizes
Make a larger mixture using 200 g (8 oz) of caster sugar, butter or margarine and flour, with 4 eggs and just over 1 tablespoon water with chosen flavourings and bake in a greased and lined deep round 20 cm (8 inch) cake tin allowing about 1 hour to cook; or in the same size square tin, which will take a little less time to cook; or in a 23 cm (9 inch) deep round tin, which should take about 45-50 minutes to cook.

Opposite, clockwise from top left: Madeira Cake baked in a loaf tin; basic Victoria Sandwich Cake; coffee-flavoured Victoria Sandwich Cake with a Coffee Butter Cream filling (see page 38)

23 cm (9 inch) round tin	28×18×4 cm (11×7×1½ inch) slab cake	23 cm (9 inch) round or petal shaped tin*	23 cm (9 inch) square tin	25 cm (10 inch) round or petal shaped tin	30×25×5 cm (12×10×2 inch) slab cake
200 g (8 oz)	200 g (8 oz)	250 g (10 oz)	250 g (10 oz)	250 g (10 oz)	250 g (10 oz)
200 g (8 oz)	200 g (8 oz)	250 g (10 oz)	250 g (10 oz)	250 g (10 oz)	250 g (10 oz)
200 g (8 oz)	200 g (8 oz)	250 g (10 oz)	250 g (10 oz)	250 g (10 oz)	250 g (10 oz)
100 g (4 oz)	100 g (4 oz)	125 g (5 oz)	125 g (5 oz)	125 g (5 oz)	125 g (5 oz)
4	4	5	5	5	5
1½ lemons	1½ lemons	2 lemons	2 lemons	2 lemons	2 lemons
1 hour and 10 minutes	1-1¼ hours	1 hour and 30-40 minutes	1 hour and 25-30 minutes	1hour and 20 minutes	1 hour and 15-20 minutes

Opposite, from top: meringue disc; nest and basket of meringue cuite; piped meringue stars, shells and bars

Meringues

There are several types of meringue but the most commonly used is called Meringue Suisse. This is made by whisking egg whites until very stiff, then whisking in half the sugar gradually and folding in the rest. This is piped or spread for discs and other shapes as well as the usual tea-time meringues. Meringue Cuite is made by heating the egg whites and sugar over a pan of gently simmering water whilst it is being whisked. The meringue is used mainly for meringue baskets and shell shapes. It will also 'hold' chopped nuts etc, baked into it.

With all meringue making the bowl and whisk must be scrupulously clean and free from all traces of grease to obtain the best results and most bulk. Weigh the sugar accurately for excess sugar will result in sticky, soggy meringues.

MERINGUE SUISSE

4 eggs (size 1 or 2)
225 g (8 oz) caster sugar

Preparation time: about 10 minutes
Cooking time: 2 hours (shells, stars, bars); 2½-3 hours (discs)
Oven: 110°C, 225°F, Gas Mark ¼

1. Separate the eggs and put the whites in a large grease-free bowl. Whisk the whites using a rotary whisk, balloon whisk or electric whisk, until the mixture is thick, white and stands in stiff peaks.
2. Whisk in half to two-thirds of the sugar about a tablespoon at a time making sure it is completely incorporated and the mixture is stiff again after each addition.
3. Using a metal spoon, fold in the remainder of the sugar, again a little at a time. The meringue is now ready to pipe or spread and should be used immediately; it will not keep before cooking.

MERINGUE SHELLS, STARS AND BARS

Makes 24-36, depending on size and shape

1. Line 2 baking sheets with non-stick silicone paper, waxed paper or greased greaseproof paper.
2. Fit a piping bag with a large star vegetable nozzle and fill with meringue.
3. Pipe out shell shapes, stars or whirls or any other shapes to use to decorate the top of meringue discs or to form the sides for a meringue basket. For bars, use the same nozzle and pipe out straight lines of mixture about 10-12.5 cm (4-5 inches) long or squiggle the nozzle back and forth to give zig-zag bars. Piping a continuous twisted line will give a professional-looking shaped meringue bar.

4. Bake in a preheated oven, reversing the baking sheets in the oven after an hour to give even cooking on both trays. When ready they should be crisp and dry and should peel easily away from the paper. Leave on the paper to cool, then store between sheets of greaseproof paper in an airtight container.

MERINGUE DISCS

Makes 2 circles + 6-8 individual meringues for decoration

1. Cover 2 baking sheets with non-stick silicone paper, waxed paper, or greased greaseproof paper and draw a circle of the required size on each: 20-23 cm (8-9 inch) are the usual sizes but they can be made larger if you are baking for a party. Alternatively draw 3 circles each 2.5-4 cm (1-1½ inches) smaller than the last to give graduated sizes, beginning with the largest at 18-20 cm (7-8 inches).
2. Fill a piping bag fitted with a large plain nozzle 1-2 cm (½-¾ inch) in diameter or a large star vegetable nozzle, and, beginning in the middle of the circle, pipe a continuous spiral to fill the drawn circle. Repeat with the second circle.
3. Bake in a preheated oven, reversing the sheets in the oven after each hour. Cool on the paper, then peel off and store in an airtight container.

Note: this mixture can also be used to make 3 rectangular layers. Draw rectangles of 30 × 10 cm (12 × 4 inches) on 3 lined baking sheets, pipe on the meringue in a backwards and forwards pattern and bake as for the circles.

Brown Sugar Meringues

For attractive pale brown meringues with a delicious flavour replace 50-75 g (2-3 oz) white sugar with light soft brown sugar and sift it with the caster sugar before adding to the egg whites. Bake in the same way.

Note: baked meringues of all shapes and sizes will store satisfactorily for 7-10 days before use, provided they are kept in an airtight container.

MERINGUE CUITE

Makes about 8 nests or 1 large basket

250 g (9 oz) icing sugar
4 egg whites
few drops vanilla essence

Preparation time: about 20 minutes
Cooking time: about 2 hours
Oven: 110°C, 225°F, Gas Mark ¼

1. Sift the icing sugar at least twice to ensure it is completely free of lumps.
2. Put the egg whites into a heatproof bowl and whisk until frothy.
3. Add the icing sugar and whisk until blended. Stand the bowl over a saucepan of very gently simmering water and whisk the mixture until it becomes thick, white and stands in peaks. Whisk in the essence. The meringue cuite is now ready for piping into the shape you want.
4. For meringue nests, put the meringue into a piping bag fitted with a 1 cm (½ inch) plain nozzle or a large star nozzle. Line 2 baking sheets with non-stick silicone paper and draw circles of 10-12.5 cm (4-5 inches) over them.
5. Use the meringue to fill these circles beginning in the centre of each; then pipe a ring on top of the outside of the meringue circle to form the raised sides of the nest. Alternatively, instead of the outside ring, a series of dots or rosettes may be piped around the edge of the circle.
6. Bake in the oven for about 2 hours, reversing the sheets in the oven after 1 hour. Cool on the paper before peeling off. A large basket may be made in the same way beginning with a circle of about 23-25 cm (9-10 inches) and piping at least 2 rings on top of each other to form the sides.

APRICOT GLAZE

The cooled, sieved glaze can be stored in an airtight container in the refrigerator for up to a week, but it must be boiled and cooled again before applying it to the cake. The smallest quantity you can make up is 2 tablespoons jam and 1 teaspoon water, any less is difficult to handle.

The glaze is brushed over cakes, before marzipan or fondant moulding paste is added, to hold any loose crumbs on the cake and to help stick the icing firmly in place. It is also good for joining different shaped pieces of cake together before covering them with icing, as in several of the cakes in the Novelty Cakes chapter. Apricot and other jam glazes can also be brushed over fruits in tarts to give them an attractive finish, as on the Scandinavian Plum Tart on page 81.

Makes about 5 tablespoons.

175 g (6 oz) apricot jam or preserve
2 tablespoons water

Preparation time: about 5 minutes
Cooking time: about 5 minutes

1. Put the jam into a small saucepan with the water and heat gently until the jam has completely melted, stirring occasionally.
2. Rub through a sieve and return the purée to a clean saucepan.
3. Bring back to the boil and simmer for at least 1 minute or until the required consistency is obtained. Allow to cool before use.

Glazing the prepared top of a Light Fruit Cake. Marzipan has been used to level the top of the cake

Adding Colour
To colour marzipan, simply add several drops of the chosen colour or colours, then knead and squeeze the marzipan until the colour is evenly distributed throughout with no streaking. Powder or paste colourings can be used in the same way, adding sufficient until the required colour is obtained. If the marzipan becomes a bit soft, knead in a little sifted icing sugar as well.

MARZIPAN OR ALMOND PASTE

This is used for covering all cakes to be coated with royal icing and for most cakes to be covered in fondant moulding paste, especially if a fruit cake; for decorative tops to cakes; or for moulding all sorts of shapes, such as flowers, leaves and animals.

Make up in quantities of not more than 900 g (2 lb) at a time, otherwise it becomes unmanageable. You can make up small quantities from using 50 g (2 oz) ground almonds, etc. However, if you need small amounts for colouring, it is often best to use a commercial marzipan. The remainder, if securely wrapped in polythene will keep for up to a month or so.

Marzipan does not freeze.

To make a natural-coloured marzipan, use 2 lightly beaten egg whites instead of the egg or egg yolks for mixing.

Makes 450 g (1 lb)

100 g (4 oz) caster sugar
100 g (4 oz) icing sugar, sifted
225 g (4 oz) ground almonds
1 teaspoon lemon juice
few drops almond essence
1 egg or 2 egg yolks, beaten

Preparation time: about 10 minutes

1. Combine the sugars and ground almonds and make a well in the centre.
2. Add the lemon juice, almond essence and sufficient egg or egg yolks to mix to a firm but manageable dough.
3. Turn on to a lightly sugared surface and knead until smooth. Take care not to overknead or the marzipan may begin to turn oily. (There is no remedy for this and it then becomes difficult to

MARZIPAN (approximate quantities)		
Square		15 cm (6 inch)
Round	15 cm (6 inch)	18 cm (7 inch)
Marzipan	350 g (¾ lb)	450 g (1 lb)

use.) It can be wrapped securely in polythene or kitchen foil and stored for up to 2 days before use.

Commercial marzipan is available ready to roll in the traditional yellow or 'white' which is in fact natural-coloured. They are both good and easy to use and the natural one is ideal for adding colours to for moulding as it gives truer colours than the yellow version.

How to Apply Marzipan to a Cake

The same method is used for both round and square cakes and any other shape you wish to cover. For fancy shapes, such as petal or oval, simply use the cake tin as a pattern for cutting out the top section of marzipan.

To calculate quantities for different shapes, simply calculate roughly what the finished size of the baked cake will be and allow about 100 g (4 oz) more than the amount given in the chart for a similar-sized round or square cake.

1. Place almost half of the marzipan on a working surface dredged with icing sugar, or between 2 sheets of polythene. Roll out evenly until 2.5 cm (1 inch) larger than the top of the cake.
2. Brush the top of the cake with apricot glaze (see picture, left) and if the surface is uneven or very curved, build up the edges or fill in any holes with scraps of marzipan. If the cake is very uneven, roll it out as smoothly as possible, or cut off the lumps and bumps and turn the cake upside down and cover the base with marzipan instead.
3. Invert the cake on to the marzipan and carefully turn the cake the right way up. Alternatively lift the marzipan shape on to the top of the cake keeping it even. Trim off any excess and smooth the edges with a small palette knife.

4. Stand the cake marzipan side up, on a cake board and brush the sides with apricot glaze.
5. Cut 2 pieces of string, one the exact height of the cake and the other the complete circumference. Roll out the remaining marzipan and using the string as a guide cut a strip to the height and circumference of the cake. Two shorter lengths can be cut if this is easier.
6. Loosely roll the marzipan strip(s) into a coil. Place one end on the side of the cake and unroll carefully, moulding the marzipan to the shape of the cake as you go and making sure the marzipan touches the board.
7. Using a small palette knife, smooth the join at the ends of the strip and where the strip meets the marzipan on top of the cake. If the marzipan seems unduly moist, rub all over with sifted icing sugar, and brush off the surplus.
8. Store the cake, uncovered, in a warm and dry, but not too hot, place for at least 24 hours before applying any icing. For tiered wedding cakes and those which you want to keep for a while after icing, allow up to a week; otherwise the oils from the marzipan will seep through into the royal icing and leave unsightly marks of discoloration.

Note: Some people prefer to add the sides of marzipan to the cake before the top; it doesn't really matter which way you do it as long as it is kept neat and even and you fill in any holes or dents before you start.

For notes on making decorative items from marzipan, see pages 44-5 (holly and mistletoe leaves and berries), 49 (fruits), 50-51 (rose buds, flowers and leaves), 130 (figures, including people and animals) and 144 (petits fours).

Inverting the cake on to the rolled-out marzipan

Shaping the marzipan round the top edge of the cake

Unrolling the marzipan strip cut to fit the side of the cake

Smoothing out the joins in the marzipan

18 cm (7 inch)	20 cm (8 inch)	23 cm (9 inch)	25 cm (10 inch)	28 cm (11 inch)	30 cm (12 inch)
20 cm (8 inch)	23 cm (9 inch)	25 cm (10 inch)	28 cm (11 inch)	30 cm (12 inch)	
575 g (1¼ lb)	800 g (1¾ lb)	900 g (2 lb)	1 kg (2¼ lb)	1.25 kg (2½ lb)	1.4 kg (3 lb)

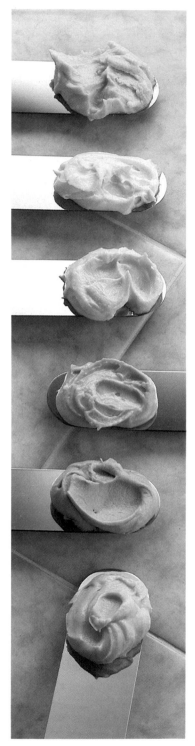

ROYAL ICING

Royal icing can be made in any quantity as long as you allow 1 egg white to each 225 g (8 oz) icing sugar. However, it is better to make up not more than a 900 g (2 lb) quantity of icing at a time because the icing keeps better if made in small quantities. It is difficult to make up much less than 1 egg white quantities, although it is possible to use ½ egg white and 100 g (4 oz) icing sugar.

The icing can be stored in an airtight container in a cool place for about 2 days. However, it must be stirred very thoroughly before use, and if necessary a little extra sifted icing sugar added to correct the consistency which often seems to soften if the icing is left to stand for more than a few hours.

While using the icing, cover the bowl with a damp cloth to prevent a skin forming. Egg albumen powder, available from specialist cake decorating shops, can be made up according to the instructions on the packet and used in place of fresh egg whites.

Glycerine can be added to help soften the icing and make cutting easier. It should be omitted from the icing for the first 2 coats on the top surface of the bottom tier of a wedding cake and the first coat on the top surface of the middle tier, as a hard surface is needed to take the weight of other tiers. It should be used carefully as too much glycerine will make a very soft icing.

Makes 675 g (1½ lb)

3 egg whites
approx. 675 g (1½ lb) icing sugar, sifted
3 teaspoons strained lemon juice
1-1½ teaspoons glycerine (optional)

Preparation time: about 15 minutes, plus standing

1. Put the egg whites into a clean, grease-free bowl and beat until frothy. Using a wooden spoon, gradually beat in half the sifted icing sugar. (A hand-held electric mixer can be used but it will incorporate a lot of air and the resulting bubbles will be difficult to disperse.)
2. Add the lemon juice, glycerine and half the remaining sugar. Beat well until smooth and very white.
3. Gradually beat in enough of the remaining icing sugar to give a consistency which will just stand in soft peaks.
4. Put the icing into an airtight container or cover the bowl with a damp cloth and leave to stand for an hour or so, if possible, to allow most of the air bubbles to come to the surface and burst.
5. The icing is now ready for coating a cake; or it can be thickened a little with extra sifted icing sugar for piping stars, flowers, etc; or thinned down for flooding run-outs, etc, by adding a little lightly beaten egg white or lemon juice. Several cakes in chapters 2 and 3 include decorative elements, such as flowers, fans, birds and butterflies; made from the basic white or tinted royal icing.

Colouring Icings

It is now possible to buy just about any colour and shade of liquid food colouring, or powder or paste to tint your icing any colour you may wish to. However, if you can only obtain the more basic colours, it is useful to know how to mix them to make other colours.

You get a truer colour when you are

ROYAL ICING (approximate quantities of icing sugar)						
Square		15 cm (6 inch)	18 cm (7 inch)	20 cm (8 inch)	23 cm (9 inch)	25 cm (10 inch)
Round	15 cm (6 inch)	18 cm (7 inch)	20 cm (8 inch)	23 cm (9 inch)	25 cm (10 inch)	28 cm (11 inch)
Icing sugar	450 g (1 lb)	575 g (1¼ lb)	675 g (1½ lb)	900 g (2 lb)	1 kg (2¼ lb)	1.25 kg (2½ lb)

Approximate quantities of icing sugar used to make royal icing for two thin coats on round and square cakes.

Calculate other shapes from these amounts allowing a little extra.

adding colourings to a white icing, such as royal or glacé, than you do when colouring butter creams, because they are cream coloured to start with.

It is not possible to be precise about the amount of colour to add to achieve a specific colour but do remember to add colours very sparingly; it is very easy to add more but impossible to remove the colour once added. Dip the tip of a skewer into the colouring, then add this to the icing. Continue to add colour in this way, beating the icing after each addition until the correct colour is obtained. It may take longer but is a really safe way of doing it. The colour of royal icing darkens slightly on drying.

Pink – use a pink colouring or just a minor touch of cochineal.

Peach – use peach, which may still need a touch of pink to prevent it looking too orange, or mix it with pink and yellow and possibly a touch of orange.

Cream – a touch of a golden rather than a primrose yellow with a touch of pink and/or orange.

Red – you really need a paste or powder colouring to achieve a true red.

Mauve – use a mauve colour if available but it may be a bit on the pink side, so add a touch of a true blue if necessary. You can make your own chosen shade of mauve with pink and blue but it tends to turn grey very easily.

Greens – these sometimes need a touch of blue to give a better colour, although the soft greens need only a touch of the colouring anyway.

Golden yellow – often a tiny touch of orange helps to give a warm golden yellow, be it very pale or quite deep.

Blues – bought blue colourings vary from a turquoise to almost purple, so

watch out carefully when using blue, and they again can turn grey if you are not careful.

Note: *Some people are allergic to certain artificial colours, and care should be taken in their use.*

How To Flat Ice a Cake Ready For Decoration

Some people prefer to ice the top of the cake first, then the sides; others do it the other way round. It doesn't really matter, so long as you add several thin coats rather than one thick coat, since this gives the smoothest surface. It is wise to apply the icing to one surface at a time rather than all in one go, allowing each application time to dry before continuing, or you may spoil the surface already put on the cake.

After each coat to the top or sides, it is important to pare or cut off any lumps or bumps in the icing, using a finely serrated-edge knife.

An ordinary royal iced cake requires 2 coats on the top and sides. Sometimes an extra coat on the top is necessary, if it is not as smooth as you would like. A wedding cake, however, requires 3 coats all over, with an extra coat on the top for the lower tiers, to help them hold the weight of the other cakes.

To Flat Ice The Top of a Cake

1. Attach the cake to a cake board, which is 2.5-5 cm (1-2 inches) larger than the cake, with a dab of icing. Put a quantity of icing in the centre of the cake and smooth out with a palette knife, using a paddling movement. This helps to remove air bubbles and distribute the icing evenly. Remove the surplus icing from the edges.

2. Take an icing ruler or long palette knife and draw across the cake towards you, carefully and evenly, keeping the ruler or knife at an angle of about 30°. Take care not to press too heavily or unevenly.

3. Remove surplus icing by running the palette knife (or another) around the top edge of the cake, holding it at right angles to the cake.

Using an icing ruler to smooth the royal icing on top of the cake

Removing surplus icing by running a palette knife round the top edge of the cake

28 cm (11 inch)	30 cm (12 inch)
30 cm (12 inch)	
1.4 kg (3 lb)	1.6 kg (3½ lb)

Smoothing the side icing on a cake with an icing comb

4. If not sufficiently smooth, cover with a little more icing and draw the ruler or knife across the cake again, repeating until smooth. Leave to dry.

To Flat Ice The Sides of The Cake

Place the cake on an icing turntable if possible, or use an upturned plate.

For a round cake:

1. Spread a thin but covering layer of icing all round the sides of the cake. Again use a paddling action to push out as much air as possible, keeping the icing fairly smooth.
2. Hold an icing comb or scraper or a palette knife at an angle of about 45° to the cake. Starting at the back of the cake, with your free hand slowly rotate the cake, and at the same time move the comb slowly and evenly round the sides of the cake. Remove the comb at an angle and fairly quickly, so the join is hardly noticeable.
3. Lift any excess icing from the top of the cake using a palette knife, again rotating the cake. If not sufficiently smooth, wipe the comb and repeat. Leave to dry.

For a square cake:

1. The best way of achieving good even corners is to ice 2 opposite sides first, leave to dry, then ice the other two.
2. Spread some icing on one side, then draw the comb or palette knife towards you, keeping the cake still to give an even side.
3. Cut off the icing down the corner in a straight line, also cut the surplus off the top and base of the cake.
4. Repeat with the opposite side and leave to dry.
5. Repeat the process with the 2 remaining sides, keeping the corners neat and tidy. Leave to dry.

To Ice Other Shaped Cakes

Basically cakes are shaped similar to round or square cakes. Those similar to a round cake, e.g. heart, oval, and petal are smoothed off all in one go after adding a smooth and even coating of icing all round the sides. An oval is very similar to a round; with a petal take care to dip evenly into the 'dents'.

Other shapes tend to be multi-sided, such as octagonal or hexagonal. These are iced in the same way as a square cake, adding the icing to every other side and, when dry, filling in with those not already iced.

Adding Second and Third Coats of Icing

1. Repeat the method for the top and sides when applying each subsequent coat but make sure each layer is dry before adding the next or you may disturb the previous layers. This will usually take from 3-6 hours, but can vary according to the room atmosphere.
2. Leave the cake to dry, uncovered, for 24 hours after completing the icing. The cake is now base-iced ready for the decoration.

To Ice The Cake Board

Sometimes it is a good idea to ice the cake board too, either before adding a decoration to it, or simply to cover up the expanse of silver board which some people find unsightly. To do this, first completely base ice the cake on its board and leave to dry. Then stand the cake on an icing turntable and coat the board with a thin layer of icing (it may spread more easily if thinned slightly with a little egg white or lemon juice). Either run a palette knife round the edge while revolving the cake or hold an icing comb at an angle to the icing whilst rotating. Remove surplus icing from the edge of the board with a palette knife. With a square cake use the same method but take care with the corners.

The board may also be decorated in other ways. Flowers or other decorations on the cake may be used to decorate the board, too. Piping to match that on the top edge or round the base can be added to the board. If the cake has any lace decoration on it, the board can be covered with lace icing to match.

GLACE ICING

This is the quickest of icings to make and is useful for icing sponge, sandwich and other cakes, as well as small cakes and biscuits. It cannot be used for piping stars or anything fancy. The icing will remain liquid if the bowl is placed in another large bowl containing hot water, otherwise, unless used quickly it will set in the bowl.

Cakes covered in glacé icing must not be moved until the icing has set completely or it will crack. The cake must be put on to a board which is firm enough not to bend, before the icing is added for it can't be moved after adding the icing.

Glacé icing can be coloured and flavoured in any way you like to blend with any type and coloured decoration and flavour of cake.

Make up a small quantity in the same way as a large one; if it becomes too runny simply add more icing sugar.

Glacé icing must be used at once, it does not keep. Once on the cake it will keep as long as the cake, i.e. up to 2 weeks. It is not used on rich fruit cakes.

Makes sufficient to cover the top of a 20 cm (8 inch) round cake. Use double quantities to cover the top and sides.

225 g (8 oz) icing sugar
2-4 tablespoons hot water or fruit juice
food colouring and/or flavouring
    (optional)

Preparation time: about 5 minutes

1. Sift the icing sugar into a bowl.
2. Gradually beat in sufficient water or juice to give a smooth icing, thick enough to coat the back of a spoon easily. Extra water or sugar can be added to achieve the correct consistency.
3. Add a few drops of food colouring or flavouring, if used. Use at once or place over a bowl or pan of hot water for a short period.
4. Alternatively all the ingredients can be put into a saucepan and be heated gently, stirring continuously, until well mixed and smooth; take care not to overheat or the icing will crystallize. Use very quickly.
5. If a crust begins to form on the icing before added to the cake, rub it through a sieve before use.

To Coat The Top of a Cake With Glacé Icing
1. Make sure the cake is completely ready before you begin.
2. Make the glacé icing, add colour if desired, then, when it is thick enough to coat the back of a wooden spoon, pour it over the middle of the cake. Using a round-bladed knife spread it out quickly and evenly over the top almost to the edge. If the icing drops over the edge, quickly remove it with a knife or palette knife or leave it until it has set, when it can be cut off with a sharp knife. Do not disturb it as the icing sets, or it will crack.
3. Alternatively tie a piece of non-stick silicone paper all round the sides of the cake to come about 2.5 cm (1 inch) above the top of the cake, pour on the icing, spreading it out almost to the edge. It will then run out by itself and be held in place by the paper. Prick any air bubbles that may appear and leave to set. When set, very carefully ease off the paper.
4. Either add decorations to the glacé icing as it begins to set, or wait until quite set before adding.

To coat a whole cake in glacé icing
1. It is a good idea to stand the cake on a thin cake card the exact size of the cake, as this keeps the cake rigid when it is moved and should prevent the icing from cracking. Stand the cake on a wire tray over a plate or tray.
2. Pour almost all of the icing over the middle of the cake and spread it out evenly, allowing it to run down the sides. Use a palette knife dipped in hot water to help spread the icing over the sides; fill in any gaps with the icing left in the bowl.
3. Leave to set, then trim off drips. Remove the cake carefully.

Variations:
Lemon or Orange Glacé Icing: use strained fruit juice instead of the water. A few drops of food colouring can also be used.
Coffee Glacé Icing: use a little coffee essence or very strong black coffee in place of part or all of the water.
Chocolate Glacé Icing: sift 1-2 tablespoons cocoa powder with the sugar and continue as above. A few drops of vanilla essence may also be added.
Mocha: sift 2 teaspoons cocoa powder and 1 or 2 teaspoons instant coffee powder with the sugar and continue as above. Alternatively, you could sift the cocoa with the sugar and add 1-2 teaspoons coffee essence with the water.

FONDANT MOULDING PASTE OR ICING

This icing is simple to use once you get used to its consistency. It is also easy to make, since extra sifted icing sugar can be added until it is sufficiently malleable. Use it for covering cakes either after adding a layer of marzipan to the cake, when it needs to be brushed lightly with egg white to make the ice adhere, or add it directly to the cake if it is a sponge or madeira after brushing the cake with apricot glaze.

It should be rolled out on a surface sprinkled with a mixture of sifted icing sugar and cornflour and, for ease of movement, it can be rolled out on a sheet of polythene sprinkled with the sugar mixture. To smooth it, simply rub in a circular movement (take care if you have long nails or are wearing rings) with the fingertips, which have been dipped in icing sugar and cornflour. The paste can be coloured by adding liquid or powder or paste food colourings; and flavourings can be added, too. Apart from cake covering, it is also good for moulding all types of animals, flowers and other shapes. It can be painted with liquid food colouring for extra effect.

Fondant moulding paste can be used almost interchangeably with royal icing but take care when covering tiered wedding cakes for sometimes the icing does not set hard enough to take the weight of heavy top tiers. Make sure it is given extra time for drying out (see page 37, step 6) and it may help to add 1-2 coats of royal icing to the tops of the cake before adding the moulding paste.

Liquid glucose or glucose syrup is available from most larger chemists and also from specialist cake decorating shops. A number of these are listed on page 144.

It is difficult to make up quantities of more than 900 g (2 lb) because of the kneading required. It blends most easily when made in 450-700 g (1-1½ lb) quantities. Smaller quantities can be used but the egg white and liquid glucose quantities must be weighed very accurately. If only small quantities are required, use a ready-made fondant paste, which will keep for up to a couple of months if wrapped securely in polythene. It is obtainable in supermarkets as well as specialist cake decorating shops (see page 144).

Makes 450 g (1 lb)

450 g (1 lb) icing sugar
1 egg white
50 g (2 oz) liquid glucose or glucose syrup
food colouring and/or flavouring (optional)

Preparation time: about 10-15 minutes

1. Sift the icing sugar into a mixing bowl to remove all lumps and make a well in the centre.
2. Add the egg white and liquid glucose. Beat with a wooden spoon or spatula, gradually pulling in the icing sugar from the sides of the bowl, to give a stiff mixture.
3. Knead the icing thoroughly, mixing in any remaining icing sugar in the bowl to give a smooth and manageable paste.
4. Add colouring and flavouring as desired and extra sifted icing sugar, if necessary, to obtain the correct consistency – i.e. suitable for rolling, which you will soon be able to judge with practice.
5. The icing can be stored in a tightly-sealed polythene bag or a plastic container in a cool place for 2-3 days.

FONDANT MOULDING PASTE (approximate quantities)						
Square		15 cm (6 inch)	18 cm (7 inch)	20 cm (8 inch)	23 cm (9 inch)	25 cm (10 inch)
Round	15 cm (6 inch)	18 cm (7 inch)	20 cm (8 inch)	23 cm (9 inch)	25 cm (10 inch)	28 cm (11 inch)
Moulding paste	350 g (¾ lb)	450 g (1 lb)	700 g (1½ lb)	800 g (1¾ lb)	900 g (2 lb)	1 kg (2¼ lb)

It is also possible and easy to buy ready-made fondant moulding paste from both large supermarkets and specialist icing and cake decorating shops.

How To Apply Fondant Moulding Paste to a Cake

If the cake is covered with marzipan, first brush the marzipan lightly all over with egg white.

If the cake is without marzipan, brush it first with Apricot glaze (page 30).

1. Either roll out the icing on a sheet of polythene dredged with a mixture of icing sugar and cornflour or directly on the working surface dredged with the same mixture. Make sure the rolling pin is also dredged with the icing sugar mixture. Alternatively roll it out between 2 sheets of polythene. Roll it until it is the width of the top of the cake plus the sides, plus about 2.5 cm (1 inch) extra; this usually means about 13-15 cm (5-6 inches) larger than the top of the cake.

2. Support the icing on a rolling pin, pull off the polythene, if using, and place the icing centrally over the top of the cake.

3. Press the icing on to the sides of the cake working it from the centre of the cake out to the edge, then down the sides, using your fingers (dipped in a mixture of icing sugar and cornflour) and using a circular movement to give an even covering. Trim off the excess icing from around the base of the cake using a sharp knife. Smooth out around the base and trim again if necessary. Any wrinkles or marks can be removed by rubbing over in a circular movement with the fingers.

4. For square cakes, if you want straight-edged, rather than rounded-edged corners, you can cut out a piece of icing from each corner, then mould it carefully to conceal the join. However, the joy of this icing is the 'soft' edges it gives to corners, which look so good.

5. For any other shaped cake, mould it in the same way, but if it is a difficult shape, such as a horseshoe, it will be necessary to cut the icing in one or two places to achieve a good even covering.

6. Leave for at least 24 hours to dry and preferably 2-3 days before adding the decoration.

Using Fondant Moulding Paste in Cake Decorating

As this book shows, fondant moulding paste may be used for making decorations for cakes as well as for giving it a smoothly iced surface. For examples of how the moulding paste may be used, see pages 46, 129 and 130-1 for making animals and figures such as a Santa for a Christmas cake and the angels and figures round a Nativity crib; page 47 for decorative trims such as horseshoes; page 57 for pretty frills; page 67 for moulded roses; and pages 58 and 72 for other moulded flowers.

Using a rolling pin to place the rolled-out fondant moulding paste over the top of the cake

Pressing the fondant moulding paste down round the sides of the cake

Using a sharp knife to trim off excess fondant moulding paste

28 cm (11 inch)	30 cm (12 inch)
30 cm (12 inch)	
1.25 kg (2½ lb)	1.4 kg (3 lb)

A Favourite Icing
This standard and favourite icing can be coloured and flavoured in a wide variety of ways to complement the type of cake being filled and/ or iced; it is also ideal for adding pretty but simple decorations with or without a piping bag and nozzle, on to cakes iced in butter cream or fondant moulding paste. It can be used straight on to a cake or over a layer of marzipan. If the cake to be covered in butter cream appears to be crumbly, it is best to brush it with apricot glaze first to prevent the crumbs from getting mixed into the icing. It is simple to make up half quantities of the butter cream. It will also freeze once made.

BUTTER CREAM ICING

Makes sufficient to cover the top and sides of an 18 cm (7 inch) sandwich cake; or fill and cover the top of the cake.

100 g (4 oz) butter or soft margarine
175-225 g (6-8 oz) icing sugar, sifted
few drops of vanilla essence or other flavouring (optional)
colourings (optional)
1-2 tablespoons milk, top-of-the-milk, evaporated milk or fruit juice

Preparation time: about 10 minutes

1. Cream the butter or margarine until very soft.
2. Beat in the sugar a little at a time, adding essence to taste and colouring, if liked, and sufficient milk or other liquid to give a fairly firm but spreading consistency.
3. Store in an airtight container in the refrigerator for up to a week, if wished. Allow to return to room temperature before use.
4. If using for piping lattice or writing the consistency of the icing may need a little more milk to make it flow easily without breaking. For piping with a star nozzle the consistency can be firmer.

Variations:
Coffee Butter Cream: omit the vanilla and replace 1 tablespoon of the milk with coffee essence or very strong black coffee; or beat in 2-3 teaspoons coffee powder with the icing sugar.
Chocolate Butter Cream: add 25-40 g (1-1½ oz) melted plain chocolate; or dissolve 1-2 tablespoons sifted cocoa powder in a little hot water to give a thin paste, cool and beat into the icing in place of some of the milk.
Orange or Lemon Butter Cream: omit the vanilla, replace the milk with orange or lemon juice and add the finely grated rind of 1 orange or lemon and a little orange or yellow liquid food colouring.
Mocha Butter Cream: dissolve 1-2 teaspoons cocoa powder in 1 tablespoon coffee essence or very strong black coffee and add in place of some or all the milk.
Almond Butter Cream: replace the vanilla with almond essence and beat in about 2 tablespoons very finely chopped toasted almonds if liked. A few drops of green colouring may be added to give a pale almond green coloured icing.
Apricot Butter Cream: omit the vanilla and milk and beat in 3 tablespoons sieved apricot jam, a pinch of grated lemon rind, a squeeze of lemon juice and a touch of orange liquid food colouring.
Minted Butter Cream: replace the vanilla essence with peppermint essence – but in moderation, add a few drops green food colouring and/or 3-4 crushed minted chocolate matchsticks.
Liqueur Butter Cream: omit the vanilla essence and replace the milk with brandy, whisky, rum, sherry or other liqueur. A few drops of an appropriate food colouring can be added.

CONTINENTAL BUTTER CREAM

Makes sufficient to fill and cover the top of an 18-20 cm (7-8 inch) sandwich cake.

75 g (3 oz) caster sugar
4 tablespoons water
2 egg yolks
100-175 g (4-6 oz) butter, preferably unsalted

Preparation time: about 20 minutes

1. Put the sugar into a small heavy-based saucepan with the water and mix gently over a low heat until the sugar has completely dissolved. Put a sugar thermometer into the pan and boil until it reaches the thread stage 110°C/225°F. If you do not have a thermometer, dip the back of a teaspoon in the syrup and pull the syrup sharply away with the back of another spoon. If no thread forms, boil a little more and test again.

2. Put the egg yolks into a bowl and whisk well – a hand-held electric mixer is ideal for this job. Gradually pour the syrup in a thin stream on to the eggs whilst whisking the mixture continuously.

3. Continue whisking the mixture until it is cold and thick.

4. Put the butter into another bowl and beat until soft and creamy, then beat in the whisked mixture a little at a time, until smooth and of a spreading consistency. Use at once, or add flavourings as for butter cream.

CREME PATISSIERE

Makes about 450 ml (¾ pint)

300 ml (½ pint) milk
50 g (2 oz) caster sugar
20 g (¾ oz) plain flour
15 g (½ oz) cornflour
1 egg
1 egg yolk
few drops of vanilla essence
15-25 g (½-1 oz) butter

Preparation time: about 10-15 minutes, plus cooling

1. Heat the milk gently in a saucepan but do not boil.

2. Put the sugar, flour, cornflour, egg and egg yolk into a bowl and whisk or beat until very smooth and creamy. Beat in a little of the hot milk.

3. Add the egg mixture to the rest of the milk in the pan and beat until smooth, then cook gently, stirring continuously, until the mixture thickens and comes just to the boil.

4. Add the vanilla essence and butter and cook gently over a low heat for a minute or so, still continuing to stir.

5. Remove from the heat and turn into a bowl. Cover tightly with cling film, or put a piece of wet greaseproof paper on to the surface of the custard to prevent a skin forming. The custard can be stored in the refrigerator for up to 48 hours before use, preferably in an airtight plastic container.

FUDGE FROSTING

Makes sufficient to fill and frost a 20 cm (8 inch) cake

75 g (3 oz) butter
3 tablespoons milk
25 g (1 oz) soft brown sugar
1 tablespoon black treacle
300 g (12 oz) icing sugar, sifted

1. Put the butter, milk, brown sugar and treacle in a heatproof bowl over a saucepan of hot but not boiling water. Stir occasionally until the butter and sugar have melted, then remove the bowl from the saucepan.

2. Stir in the icing sugar, then beat with a wooden spoon until the icing is smooth.

3. Pour quickly over a cake for a smooth coating, or leave to cool, then spread over the cake and swirl with a small palette knife. Leave the frosting to set, then decorate as desired.

Clockwise from top left: Crème Pâtissière; Fudge Frosting; basic Butter Cream Icing; Continental Butter Cream

39

Simply Decorated Cakes

Simplicity is the essence of the decoration of the cakes in this chapter, but the effect achieved should provide a cake that looks far more elaborate and difficult to produce than it really is. The cakes are iced in butter cream, glacé icing, royal icing and fondant moulding paste, all of which give a good basis for adding a variety of decorations.

If you are a beginner, select the cake to make after reading through the whole recipe to check that the decorations are all within your scope. Since the wording or occasion depicted on the cake can be altered to suit your particular celebration, any of the cakes featured in this chapter can be used for almost any type of occasion.

Take your time to achieve the smoothest finish possible to the base icing of the cake to be decorated, whatever type of icing is used. This takes a little practice, but all icings will hold up sufficiently to get a smooth surface before they set. The most important factor is to make the icing the correct consistency before you apply it to the cake; finding the correct consistency will come with practice.

Allow the base icing to set (or, in the case of butter cream, become firmer) before starting the decorations. The colour schemes chosen for these cakes are only suggestions and you can experiment with many other combinations. Ribbons and bought decorations or flowers must be obtained before starting the cake icing so that the icings can be tinted to match or blend with them before the cake is base iced.

If you think that some of the decorations are too difficult to make yourself, you can buy many of them from specialist cake-decorating shops; ready-made marzipan fruits, sugar flowers and leaves (or use silver or gold leaves) are all available. Horseshoes, too, can be bought in silver or gold, as can placques which say 40 Years, Happy Anniversary, Season's Greetings, etc. Where artificial flowers are suggested for decoration, small real flowers or flowers moulded from marzipan or moulding icing can be used instead.

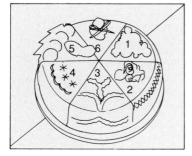

1. Decorative fruits made from marzipan
2. Moulded roses, horseshoes cut from fondant moulding paste and piped lattice decoration
3. Piped shells and lacework patterns and holly leaves and berries made from marzipan
4. Piped royal icing decorations for a wedding cake
5. Coffee butter cream and chocolate decorate this cake
6. Basket weave pattern piped in coffee-flavoured butter cream

HEART-SHAPED BIRTHDAY CAKE

1 × 20-23 cm (8-9 inch) round Quick
    Mix Cake (pages 22-3) *or* Madeira
    Cake (pages 26-7) cut to a heart
    shape (see page 9) or baked in a
    heart-shaped tin
6-8 tablespoons lemon curd (for Quick
    Mix Cake only)
round or heart-shaped cake board
1 quantity Apricot Glaze (page 30)
pink food colouring
1½ quantities Butter Cream (page 38)
silver balls
about 3-4 fresh flowers
6-7 silver leaves

Preparation time: to make and bake
cake and about an hour for decoration

1. If using a quick mix cake, cut it in
half horizontally, spread with the
lemon curd and reassemble. Stand on a
round or heart-shaped board about
5 cm (2 inches) larger than the cake.
The madeira cake is not filled.
2. Brush the cake all over with apricot
glaze.
3. Add a few drops of pink colouring
to the butter cream to tint it pale pink
and use about three-quarters of it to
mask the whole cake.
4. Stand the cake on an icing turntable
or plate balanced on an upturned plate.
Take a serrated-edged icing comb and
carefully pull around the sides of the
cake, at the same time moving it up and
down evenly to give a wavy line.
5. Next take a serrated-edged ruler and
pull over the top of the cake, again
moving backwards and forwards to
give a wavy line. The comb may be
used in place of a ruler but may need to
be pulled across 2 or 3 times to cover
the whole top of the cake.
Alternatively, the top may be levelled
with a small round-bladed palette knife
in a backwards and forwards
movement to give a smooth surface to
the top of the cake.
6. Tint the rest of the butter cream a
deeper shade of pink with more food
colouring. Put some into a piping bag

fitted with a plain writing nozzle (No.
2 or 3) and write the words 'Happy
Birthday' across the top of the cake.
7. Put the rest of the butter cream into
a piping bag fitted with a medium star
nozzle and pipe a continuously twisted
coil evenly around the top edge of the
cake.
8. Using the same nozzle pipe a star to
attach the cake to the board but so it
extends a little way up the side of the
cake. Pipe a normal star next to it and
continue all round the base in this way.
Top each of the small stars with a silver
ball.
9. Arrange sprays of fresh flowers on
top of the cake around the writing and
complete the decoration with a few
silver leaves.

Left: Heart-shaped Birthday
Cake; right: Basket of
Chocolates

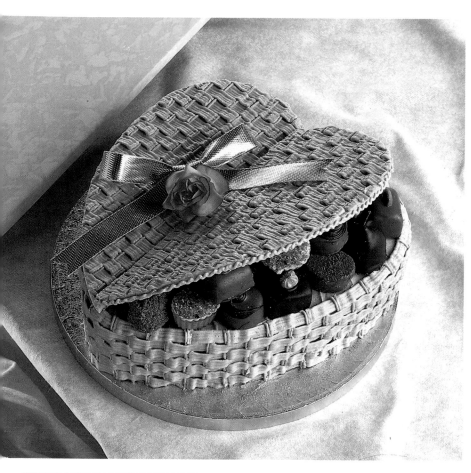

The first step in making the basket weave pattern

Building up the basket weave pattern round the cake

BASKET OF CHOCOLATES

1 × 20-23 cm (8-9 inch) heart-shaped
   Quick Mix Cake (pages 22-3) or
   Madeira Cake (pages 26-7) (baked in
   a heart-shaped tin or cut to shape, see
   page 9)
brown food colouring
about 175 g (6 oz) Fondant Moulding
   Paste (page 36)
round or heart-shaped heavy, silver
   cake board
1 quantity Apricot Glaze (page 30)
1-2 tablespoons coffee essence
   (optional)
2 quantities Butter Cream (page 38)
about 350 g (¾ lb) assorted luxury
   chocolates
large gold bow
artificial flower

Preparation time: to make the cake,
icing etc and about 1 hour for the final
decoration

1. Make the cake. Add a touch of
brown food colouring to the fondant
paste to tint it to a pale coffee colour.
Roll out the paste and cut to a heart
shape the same size as the cake. Cut in
half down the centre, place on a sheet
of non-stick silicone paper and leave to
dry in a warm place.
2. Stand the cake on a gold board
about 5 cm (2 inches) larger than the
cake. Brush all over with apricot glaze.
3. Add a touch of brown food
colouring or coffee essence to tint the
butter cream a pale coffee colour to
match the lid. Spread a thin layer over
the top of the cake and neaten with a
palette knife.
4. To work the basket weave, fit 1
piping bag with a basket weave nozzle
and another with a No. 2 writing
nozzle and fill both with butter cream.
Beginning at the dent at the back of the
cake and holding the basket weave
nozzle at an angle to the cake, pipe 3 or
more lines about 2.5 cm (1 inch) long,
one above the other and with the width
of the nozzle left between them. Next,
with the writing nozzle pipe a straight
vertical line down the edge of the
horizontal ribbon lines. Next, take the
basket nozzle again and pipe more lines
the same length as the first ones to fill
the gaps but beginning halfway along
those already piped and covering the
straight lines. Pipe another straight
vertical line down the edge and
continue to build up the basket weave
around the sides of the cake in this way
but taking care to keep it even.
5. Work basket weave in the same way
on the dried fondant paste heart pieces
for the lid, and pipe a squiggly line on
the edge. Leave to dry.
6. Arrange chocolates (in their paper
cases if preferred) around the top edge
of the cake. Build up with more
chocolates on the front half of the cake,
but leave the centre empty.
7. Carefully place the lids on the cake
sticking the cut edge into the centre
and allowing the lids to rest on the
chocolates as if they are peeping out.
Place the gold ribbon bow and the
flower in the centre of the lid.

ROUND CHRISTMAS CAKE

Left: Round Christmas Cake with lacework icing pattern; right: Square Christmas Cake with ribbon decoration

1 × 20 cm (8 inch) round Rich Fruit Cake (pages 18-19)
1 quantity Apricot Glaze (page 30)
750 g (1½ lb) Marzipan (page 30)
25 cm (10 inch) round cake board
900 g (2 lb) sugar quantity Royal Icing (page 32) or 750 g (1½ lb) Fondant Moulding Paste (page 36)
little egg white if using fondant paste
red and green food colourings

Preparation time: to make, bake, marzipan and ice the cake and make decorations plus about 1 hour for final decorations

1. Brush the cake with apricot glaze and use 575 g (1¼ lb) marzipan to cover the cake (see page 31). Stand on the cake board and leave to dry.
2. Flat ice the cake with the royal icing (see page 32) giving it 2 coats all over and a third on top (see pages 33-4) and allowing it to dry between each coat. Alternatively, brush the marzipan with egg white and cover with fondant moulding paste (see page 37). Leave to dry completely – 24 hours for royal icing and up to 48 hours for moulding paste.

3. Divide the remaining marzipan in half and colour one portion red with food colouring and the other half dark green, kneading to give even colouring. Use some of the red marzipan to make 40 holly berries.
4. Roll out the remaining red marzipan and cut to a 7.5 cm (3 inch) square. Place on non-stick silicone paper with the holly berries and dry in a warm place.
5. Roll out the green marzipan thinly and cut into 20-30 holly leaves using a special cutter of about 2.5-4 cm (1-1½ inches) in length. Mark a vein down the centre, then put each leaf over a wooden spoon handle to curve it. Leave to dry for at least 24 hours, so that the colouring will not seep on to the top of the cake and mark it.
6. To make a template for the top of the cake, cut a circle of thick paper about 1 cm (½ inch) smaller than the top of the cake. Fold it in half, then carefully into three, making sure each piece is exactly even. Draw a curve across the folds.
7. For the sides cut a strip of paper long enough to reach right round the outside of the cake and the same depth of the cake. Fold it evenly into 6. Cut 1 cm (½ inch) off the top, then make a curved cut like that on the cake top.

Making holly leaves
If you don't have a leaf cutter make your own by cutting the marzipan into rectangles about 2.5-4 cm (1-1½ inches) long and 2 cm (¾ inch) wide. Using a tiny round cutter or the base of a piping nozzle, take cuts out of the edges to make the leaf shape. Set the leaves aside to dry.

8. Place the template on the top of the cake. Put some royal icing into a piping bag fitted with a medium star nozzle and pipe a row of small shells to outline the template but not touching it. Leave to dry, then remove the template.

9. Put the side template around the side of the cake, so that it matches the top design, attaching it with a dab of icing. Pipe a similar row of shells to outline the top edge of this template. Remove and allow to dry.

10. Using a slightly larger star nozzle, put some more royal icing into a piping bag. Pipe a row of medium to large shells around the base of the cake.

11. Put some more icing into a piping bag fitted with a No. 2 writing nozzle (or a finer No. 1 nozzle if you prefer) and pipe a 'lace' design between the icing shells made with the templates to fill in the shapes. This is done by moving the nozzle back and forth to give a lacy uneven pattern.

12. Attach the square of red marzipan centrally to the top of the cake with a dab of icing, then, using a No. 2 writing nozzle, pipe a suitable Christmas message, such as the words 'Season's Greetings', on top.

13. Decorate the cake with holly leaves and berries. Leave to dry.

SQUARE CHRISTMAS CAKE

1 × 20 cm (8 inch) square Rich Fruit Cake (pages 18–19)
1 quantity Apricot Glaze (page 30)
800 g (1¾ lb) Marzipan (page 30)
25 cm (10 inch) square cake board
900 g (2 lb) Fondant Moulding Paste (page 36)
little egg white
icing sugar and cornflour for dusting
approx. 20 green mistletoe leaves, 20 natural marzipan mistletoe berries and 4 green marzipan holly leaves (see hint boxes, left and right)
450 g (1 lb) sugar quantity Royal Icing (page 32)
approx. 1¾ metres (1¾ yards) × 2 cm (¾ inch) wide red or green ribbon

Preparation time: to make, bake, marzipan and ice the cake and make the decorations plus about ¾ hour for the final decoration

1. Brush the cake with apricot glaze and use the marzipan to cover the cake (see page 31). Stand on the board and leave to dry.

2. Brush the marzipan with egg white. Roll out the fondant paste and use to cover the cake (see page 37). Mould it to fit the cake and give a rounded edge to the top edge (not the sharp edge achieved with royal icing). Trim off around the base and smooth all over with fingers dipped in icing sugar and cornflour. Leave to dry for 24-48 hours.

3. Make the holly and mistletoe leaves and berries and leave to dry.

4. Make up the royal icing. Lay the ribbon over one corner of the cake, then take it down to the base at the centre of the cake on the board and attach with a pin and a dab of icing. Take it up to the next corner and so on all round the cake.

5. Using a palette knife, add a thin layer of royal icing to the corners of the cake up to the ribbon and over the top edge corners of the cake. Pull the icing up into peaks using the palette knife or a spoon handle. Take care not to get any icing on to the ribbon. Leave to dry. Also add rough icing to cover the cake board to the edge. The rough icing may be added before the ribbon if liked.

6. Put the remaining royal icing into a piping bag fitted with a No. 2 writing nozzle and pipe a continuous circle (or square with rounded corners) or loops inside the ribbon on top of the cake. Leave to dry.

7. Attach a decoration of holly leaves and mistletoe berries and leaves to the centre of the cake with small dabs of icing .

8. Finally add bunches of 3 mistletoe leaves and some berries to the cake board where the ribbon meets it, attaching with icing and removing the pins from the ribbon.

The first step in attaching the ribbon to the Square Christmas Cake

The ribbon, attached right round the cake, has tie ends in the centre of one side

Making mistletoe leaves and berries
Use approximately 100 g (4 oz) natural marzipan to make leaves and berries.

Take a small quantity of natural marzipan to make mistletoe berries, then colour the remainder a pale green. Roll out thinly and cut into elongated leaves with rounded ends 2.5–4 cm (1–1½ inches) long. Mark a vein down the centre and leave to dry. Use any scraps to make holly leaves.

CHRISTENING CAKE

1 × 20 cm (8 inch) petal-shaped Rich
  Fruit Cake (pages 18-19) or 23 cm
  (9 inch) round cake (see page 9)
1 quantity Apricot Glaze (page 30)
700 g (1½ lb) Marzipan (page 30)
25 cm (10 inch) round cake board
800 g (1¾ lb) Fondant Moulding Paste
  (page 36)
little egg white
green, yellow, pink or blue food
  colourings
icing sugar and cornflour for dusting
15 cm (6 inch) piece of ribbon, 3 mm
  (⅛ inch) wide (optional)
225 g (8 oz) sugar quantity Royal Icing
  (page 32)
3 white or silver and white artificial
  flowers
6 silver leaves

Preparation time: to make, bake,
marzipan and ice the cake, make
decorations and about 1 hour for final
decoration

1. Brush the cake with apricot glaze
and use the marzipan to cover the cake
(see page 31). Press the long side strip
evenly into the indents as you go. Cut
the top piece using the cake tin as a
guide. Stand on the cake board and
leave to dry.
2. Reserve about 75 g (3 oz) of the
fondant paste and colour the remainder
a pale shade of green, yellow, pink or
blue, kneading until evenly blended.
3. Brush the marzipan with egg white.
Roll out the coloured fondant paste and
use to cover the cake, moulding it to fit
over the edge and into the indents
without leaving any air bubbles. Trim
off the edges, smooth with the fingers
dipped in icing sugar and cornflour and
leave to dry for 24-48 hours.
4. Use the white fondant paste to make
a teddy bear, shaping the pieces as in
the photograph (right). Join the pieces
together with dabs of water and leave
to dry. When dry, a tiny bow of
narrow ribbon the same colour as the
cake may be tied around the neck.
5. Draw a circle of 14 cm (5½ inches)

on a piece of card, cut it out and
position centrally on top of the cake.
Cut another one 2.5 cm (1 inch)
smaller in diameter and another one
2.5 cm (1 inch) smaller than that to
give 3 graduated sizes of circles.
6. Make up the royal icing, leave it
white and put some in a piping bag
fitted with a No. 2 writing nozzle.
Carefully pipe a line all round the
outside of the largest template. Allow
to dry and remove the card.
7. Put the second template inside the
piped circle of icing. Put a little icing in
a piping bag fitted with a small star
nozzle and pipe a small circle of shells
all around the outside of the template.
Allow to dry and remove the card.
8. Put the smallest template in the
centre of the cake and pipe another
plain circle using the writing nozzle.
Allow to dry and remove the card.
9. Using the star nozzle, pipe a border
of stars all round the base of the cake.
Next pipe a second star above every
third star and then a smaller one still
above this. Leave to dry.
10. Using the writing nozzle, work a
loop from the tip of one of the stars on
the side of the cake to the next and
continue all round the base. Do not
make the loops too tight or too loose or
they will break.
11. Pipe a small dot directly above the
joins of the loop near the top edge of
the cake (just over the side). Work dots
all round it, then a row of loops from
dot to dot. Allow to dry.
12. Put another row of dots in between
the first ones and work a second row of
loops over the first ones to give an
alternate looped pattern. Allow to dry.
13. Complete by working a dot on the
join of the top row of loops and
another one just above it on the side of
the cake.
14. Still using the writing nozzle, pipe
the name of the baby across the circle in
the middle of the cake just below the
centre. Attach the teddy bear above it
with a dab of icing.
15. Arrange the flowers and silver leaves
in every alternate scallop, attaching
with a dab of icing. Leave to dry.

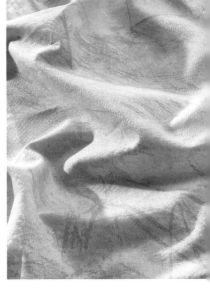

Left: Christening Cake; right:
Congratulations Cake

The Teddy Bear: the shapes
used to make the body, arms
and head of the bear and
(right) the assembled bear

Preparation time: to make, bake, marzipan (if a fruit cake) and ice the cake and about 1 hour for final decoration, plus drying

1. Brush the cake all over with apricot glaze and, if using a fruit cake, cover with marzipan, stand on the board and leave to dry.
2. Colour 100 g (4 oz) of the fondant moulding paste peach using yellow and pink or peach food colourings. Colour the rest of the paste a creamy colour with a little yellow and a touch of pink or peach. Roll out and cover the cake, brushing the marzipan first with egg white. Trim off the surplus and smooth all over with fingers dipped in icing sugar and cornflour.
3. Roll out the peach fondant and cut out 20 horseshoe shapes 3 cm (1¼ inches) high. Place on non-stick silicone paper, mark the 'nail' holes with a skewer and leave to dry.
4. Make up the butter cream and colour it a peach colour to match the horseshoes. Put some into a piping bag fitted with a No. 3 or 4 writing nozzle and pipe a series of dots all around the base of the cake. Pipe a second dot above every alternate dot.
5. Put some butter cream into a piping bag fitted with a No. 2 writing nozzle and pipe a zig-zag of icing from top dot to lower dot and back again all round the base.
6. Using the larger writing nozzle, write 'Congratulations' in butter cream evenly around the top of the cake.
7. Take the smaller writing nozzle and pipe a slanting line over the top edge of the cake all the way round, then turn the cake and pipe a second line to stretch across the edge to join up every alternate existing line to give a lattice effect. Neaten off with a dot where the lines meet.
8. Attach 'couples' of horseshoes around the sides with butter cream.
9. Make the peach roses and rosebuds, coloured to match the horseshoes. Arrange a spray of roses and silver leaves at each end of the writing, attaching with butter cream. Leave to dry.

CONGRATULATIONS CAKE

1 × 23-25 cm (9-10 inch) round Rich Fruit Cake (pages 18-19) or Madeira Cake (pages 26-7) cut to a horseshoe (page 9) or baked in a horseshoe tin
1 quantity Apricot Glaze (page 30)
800 g (1¾ lb) Marzipan (for fruit cake only), (page 30)
30 cm (12 inch) round silver cake board
1 kg (2¼ lb) Fondant Moulding Paste (page 36)
yellow, peach and pink food colourings
little beaten egg white (for fruit cake)
icing sugar and cornflour
1 quantity Butter Cream (page 38)
6-8 large peach moulded roses (see Ruby Wedding Cake – page 51)
5-6 medium peach moulded roses
4-5 peach rose buds
about 6 silver leaves

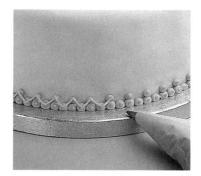

Piping the dot and zig-zag pattern round the base of the Congratulations Cake

MOTHER'S DAY CAKE

4-egg quantity chocolate Victoria
   Sandwich cake mixture (page 27)
2 quantities coffee Butter Cream (page
   38)
225 g (8 oz) plain block chocolate
23 cm (9 inch) cake board
2-3 artificial flowers

Preparation time: about 45 minutes
Cooking time: about 40 minutes
Oven: 190°C, 375°F, Gas
              Mark 5

1. Make up the mixture and place in
three 20 cm (8 inch) round sandwich
tins, greased and base-lined with greased,
grease-proof paper. Bake in a preheated
oven for 20 minutes or until well risen
and firm to the touch. Turn out and
cool on a wire tray. Remove paper.
2. Make up the coffee butter cream. Use
some to sandwich the cakes together.
3. Spread a layer of coffee butter cream
over the top of the cake and use a
round-bladed knife to smooth the top
with a backwards and forwards action.
Turn the cake at right angles to the first
lines and pull the same knife straight
across in 7 or 8 equidistant lines to
complete the pattern.
4. Using a potato peeler, pare off mini
chocolate curls from the block of
chocolate using about 150 g (5 oz) of it.
5. Spread a thin layer of butter cream
around the sides of the cake and
carefully press on the chocolate curls,
using a palette knife. Stand the cake on
the board.
6. Melt the rest of the chocolate in a
basin over a pan of hot water or in a
microwave set on cool. Take about 10
clean, dry and unblemished rose leaves
and paint the underside of each with
melted chocolate. Leave to dry, add a
second coat and chill thoroughly.
7. Attach a sheet of non-stick silicone
paper to a board, then spread out the
rest of the chocolate on it. Leave until
set but not quite dry, then, using a
sharp knife and ruler, cut it into strips
about 4 cm (1½ inches) wide. Quickly
cut these into squares, then cut again to

make into triangles. Leave to dry and
set completely. Reserve the chocolate
trimmings.
8. Melt the trimmings and put into a
greaseproof piping bag. Cut off the tip
and write 'Mother' across the cake.
9. Put some butter cream in a piping
bag fitted with a large star nozzle and
pipe a continuous twisted line of icing
all around the top of the cake about
2.5 cm (1 inch) in from the edge.
10. Carefully separate the chocolate
into triangles and stick one between
each of the butter cream whirls on top
of the cake.
11. Peel the real rose leaves carefully
from the chocolate ones and arrange
the latter with the artificial flowers in
front of 'Mother'. Leave to set.

Left: Mother's Day Cake;
right: Feathered Birthday Cake

Using a skewer to draw the
second line of the pattern on
the Feathered Birthday Cake

FEATHERED BIRTHDAY CAKE

1 × 20 cm (8 inch) round Quick Mix (pages 22-3) or Madeira Cake (pages 26-7)

1 or 1½ quantities vanilla Butter Cream (page 38)

25 cm (10 inch) round cake board

75 g (3 oz) coconut strands or desiccated coconut, toasted

glacé icing made using 225 g (8 oz) icing sugar (page 35)

green food colouring

glacé icing made using 50 g (2 oz) icing sugar (page 35)

25 g (1 oz) Marzipan (page 30)

selection of marzipan fruits, using 225 g (8 oz) Marzipan (page 30)

Preparation time: to make and bake the cake, to make and dry the marzipan fruits and about 45 minutes for the final decoration

1. If using a quick mix cake, fill it with butter cream; if madeira, leave it plain. Stand the cake on the cake board or a plate.

2. Make up the larger quantity of glacé icing and tint it a pale green with a touch of green food colouring. Immediately make up the smaller amount, colour it a deep green and put it into a greaseproof paper icing bag.

3. Pour the pale green icing over the middle of the cake and, using a palette knife, spread it out quickly so that it almost reaches the edge (it will run to the edge by itself).

4. Immediately cut the tip off the icing bag and pipe straight lines across the top of the cake at 1-2 cm (½-¾ inch) intervals. Immediately draw a skewer or the point of a knife at right angles across the lines about 2.5 cm (1 inch) apart. Turn the cake round and quickly draw the skewer across again in between the first lines but in the opposite direction to complete the feathered effect. Leave to set.

5. Trim off any excess icing and spread the sides of the cake with butter cream and coat evenly with coconut.

6. Colour the marzipan a deep green using food colouring and roll out thinly. Cut into a shape approx 6 cm (2½ inches) square with concave sides and position centrally on the cake.

7. Put a little of the butter cream into a piping bag fitted with a No. 2 or 3 writing nozzle and pipe the words 'Happy Days' on top of the marzipan.

8. Put the rest of the butter cream into a piping bag fitted with a medium star nozzle and pipe stars around the top edge of the cake.

9. Work a continuous twisted piped row of butter cream around the base of the cake.

10. Complete the decoration by adding a circle of marzipan fruits around the top of the cake, attaching with butter cream.

Making marzipan fruits

Bananas Roll a little yellow marzipan into a banana shape. Paint on stripes and markings with food colouring or gravy browning.

Pears Form natural-coloured marzipan into a pear shape. Add a stem and calyx using a clove cut in half with the tip for the stem and the head for the calyx. Paint the pear with green and brown food colourings.

Apples Roll natural-coloured or pale green marzipan into small balls with indentations at top and base. Add stems and calyx as for the pears. If using green marzipan, paint part of the apple with red food colouring. With natural-coloured marzipan, paint first with red, then blend in green colouring.

Strawberries Mould deep pink or red marzipan into a strawberry shape. Roll in granulated sugar for seeds and make a hull from green marzipan.

Oranges and Lemons Use orange and yellow marzipan. To achieve the texture of the skin either prick all over with a pin head or roll on the side of a grater. Add the tops of cloves or scraps of green marzipan for the calyx.

Grapes Make tiny balls of pale green or mauve marzipan and stick together to form bunches.

Plums Use deep yellowish-red or deep plum-mauve coloured marzipan. Make an indentation down one side of the fruit.

RUBY WEDDING CAKE

6-egg quantity vanilla Victoria
  Sandwich mixture (page 27)
1½ quantities Chocolate Butter Cream
  (page 38)
1 quantity Chocolate Glacé icing (page
  35)
75 g (3 oz) flaked almonds, toasted
33 × 23 cm (13 × 9 inch) rectangular
  cake board
about 20 red marzipan moulded roses
  (see right)
about 15 green marzipan leaves (see
  right)

Preparation time: about 1 hour
Oven: 190°C, 375°F, Gas
                             Mark 5

1. Grease and line 2 rectangular tins 28
× 18 × 4 cm (11 × 7 × 1½ inches).
Make up the cake mixture and divide
between the 2 tins. Bake in a preheated
oven for about 35 minutes until well
risen, golden brown and firm to the
touch. Turn out on to a wire tray and
leave to cool.

2. Trim off the paper and sandwich the
cakes together with some butter cream.
3. Tie a strip of double foil or
greaseproof paper round the sides of
the cake, so that it comes about 2.5 cm
(1 inch) above the top of the cake.
4. Make up the glacé icing and pour on
the cake. Spread it out evenly and burst
any air bubbles with a pin. Leave to set,
then remove the paper.
5. Spread a thin layer of butter cream
around the sides of the cake and press
the toasted almonds all over the sides.
Place on the cake board.
6. Put some butter cream in a piping
bag fitted with a No. 2 or 3 writing
nozzle and pipe 'Happy Anniversary'
and '40 years' on the cake.
7. Next put some butter cream into a
piping bag fitted with a medium star
nozzle and pipe a top edge border of
shells all around.
8. Pipe a border all around the base of
the cake with shells of alternating sizes.
9. Put sprays of red marzipan roses and
leaves on top of the cake and centrally
at the base of the sides, attaching with
butter cream. Leave to set.

Left: Ruby Wedding Cake;
right: One-Tier Wedding Cake

**Making marzipan or
moulding paste leaves**
Colour a little marzipan
or moulding paste with
green and possibly a
touch of blue liquid food
colouring to give a good
leaf colour. Knead until
evenly coloured. If it
becomes sticky, knead in
a little sifted icing sugar.
Roll out thinly and cut
out rose leaf shapes with
a sharp knife. If you can't
do this freehand, cut out
a leaf shape from card
and use this as a guide.
Using a sharp knife,
mark a main vein and
side veins on the leaf and
put to dry on non-stick
silicone paper. If curved
leaves are preferred, lay
them over a wooden
spoon handle to dry
completely.

Making marzipan or moulding paste roses

225 g (8 oz) marzipan or moulding paste will make approximately 30 roses. Colour the marzipan or moulding paste a deep ruby red (or any other colour you require) by kneading in liquid food colourings. Roll out some of the icing very thinly and cut into circles of 1-2 cm (½-¾ inch) diameter. Taking one circle at a time, hold at one side and with the fingers of the other hand carefully press out the circle until very thin and almost transparent. If necessary dip your fingers in cornflour to prevent sticking. Roll the first one up for the centre and wrap a second petal around it fairly tightly at the base, but leaving it looser at the top to show the centre. This makes a rose bud. Continue to make 2 more petals in the same way, each a fraction larger than the last, and attach in the same way, adding a dab of water if necessary to make it stick. Fold the outer petals outwards slightly. This will make a medium-sized rose. Continue adding 2 or 3 more petals, each a fraction larger than the last, to give a large rose. It may be necessary to trim off the base of the rose. The roses can be made up to 1 month before required, but should be left uncovered in a warm dry place.

ONE TIER WEDDING CAKE

1 × 25 cm (10 inch) square Rich Fruit Cake (pages 18-19)
1 quantity Apricot Glaze (page 30)
1 kg (2¼ lb) Marzipan (page 30)
30 cm (12 inch) square cake board
1.1 kg (2½ lb) Fondant Moulding Paste (page 36)
icing sugar and cornflour for rolling
little egg white for attaching icing
450 g (1 lb) sugar quantity Royal Icing (page 32)
blue food colouring
approx. 1½ metres (1½ yards) narrow 5 mm (¼ inch) blue ribbon
blue ribbons for centrepiece
small white artificial flowers (optional)

Preparation time: to make, bake, marzipan, and base ice the cake plus about 1½ hours for decoration

1. Brush the cake with apricot glaze and cover with marzipan (see page 31). Stand on the cake board and leave to dry.
2. Roll out the fondant moulding paste on a surface dredged with a mixture of sifted icing sugar and cornflour or between 2 sheets of polythene to a square about 35 cm (14 inches) wide.
3. Brush the marzipan all over with egg white, then use the fondant paste to cover the cake (see page 37). Trim off the surplus and make sure the icing is quite smooth by rubbing all over in a circular movement with the fingers dipped in icing sugar and cornflour. Leave to dry for at least 48 hours.
4. Make up the royal icing and add a touch of the blue food colouring to half of it to tint it blue.
5. Put some of the white icing into a piping bag fitted with a No. 3 plain writing nozzle and pipe plain dots all round the base of the cake to attach it to the board, then pipe a slightly smaller dot above alternate dots. Next, using a No. 2 writing nozzle, pipe an even smaller dot above those to give a line of three graduated dots all round the cake up the side of the cake. Leave to dry.

6. Fill a piping bag fitted with a No. 1 writing nozzle and blue icing, then overpipe a dot on each single dot.
7. Place the narrow ribbon around the cake, so that it sits just above the base border, attaching it with a dab of icing and a pin. (Remove the pin when dry.)
8. Put some white icing into a piping bag fitted with a No. 1 plain writing nozzle and pipe a continuous line of shallow loops all round the top edge of the cake but so that they hang just over the edge on to the sides of the cake. When dry, add a second row of loops just underneath.
9. Pipe 3 or 5 tiny dots of blue icing in the curve of each loop.
10. Using the same nozzle, pipe squiggly 'V' shapes under the join of each alternate loop all round the cake, making sure they are quite even on each corner.
11. Pipe a dot for the centre to each daisy below each of the squiggles, then add 7-8 small short lines from the centre for the petals.
12. Cut a piece of card to make a curve with loops to fit into the corner of the cake but keeping it about 4 cm (1½ inches) from the edge. Position the card in one corner and pipe a line of curved loops all around it as in the picture, using white icing. Repeat with the other 3 corners, then pipe a second loop outside the first as on the sides.
13. Pipe 3 or 4 or 5 small daisies (as on the sides) in this decoration.
14. Finally in the gaps between the corners mark a line about 5 cm (2 inches) long and pipe a squiggly 'V' line on the sides. To mark make a minute dot with the writing nozzle. Work another one above it about 2.5 cm (1 inch) long and another above that of 1 cm (½ inch) long. Leave to dry.
15. Complete the decoration by adding a blue ribbon bow to the centre of the cake. Small white artificial flowers may be added, if liked.

Elaborate Cakes

Cakes in this chapter require a certain degree of skill combined with plenty of time and patience. They are all fruit cakes covered first in marzipan and then either with royal icing or fondant moulding paste. Make all the decorations before you begin the icing, so they have time to dry out sufficiently before moving them to attach to the cake.

With these special cakes it is essential to bake a good even-shaped cake which is then covered evenly in marzipan to make it as easy as possible to add a really flat base icing. When using fondant moulding paste the top edge is usually rounded rather than straight angled (as with royal icing).

With celebration cakes it is important to know how many people a cake will feed. As a rough guide, a 450 g (1 lb) baked rich fruit cake without marzipan or icing should cut into about 10 portions when completed. Therefore, for every 45-50 people you will need about 2.25 kg (5 lb) basic cake. With a wedding cake, if the top tier is to be saved for a later occasion, the amount of cake needed must be calculated without its weight. Square cakes usually weigh heavier than round ones of the same size, although the depths can also vary slightly.

Sizes and portions for two-tier cakes
(the top tier weight included)
30 and 20 or 18 cm
(12 and 8 or 7 inch):   160-200 portions;
28 and 18 cm
(11 and 7 inch):   125-140 portions;
25 and 18 or 15 cm
(10 and 7 or 6 inch): up to 100 portions;
23 and 15 cm
(9 and 6 inch):   up to 75 portions.

Sizes and portions for three-tier cakes
(top tier weight *not* included)
30, 23 and 15 cm
(12, 9 and 6 inch):   up to 250 portions;
28, 20 and 13 cm
(11, 8 and 5 inch):   up to 150 portions;
25, 20 and 15 cm
(10, 8 and 6 inch):   up to 120 portions;
23, 18 and 13 cm
(9, 7 and 5 inch):   up to 90 portions.

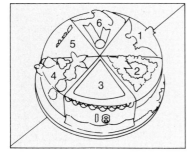

1. Fine lacework and piped butterfly and flowers, all using royal icing
2. Flowers and leaves piped with royal icing and a frill made from fondant moulding paste
3. Trellis work, curtain work and loops piped in royal icing
4. Decorative flowers made from fondant moulding paste
5. Delicate fans made with royal icing and using a fine writing nozzle
6. Decorative twisted scallops piped with a medium star nozzle

CHRISTENING CAKE

1 × 20 cm (8 inch) round Rich Fruit
  Cake (pages 18–19) or Rich Fruit
  Cake with Sherry (pages 20–1)
1 quantity Apricot Glaze (page 30)
575 g (1¼ lb) Marzipan (page 30)
25 cm (10 inch) round silver cake board
little egg white (if using moulding
  paste)
800 g (1¾ lb) Fondant Moulding Paste
  (page 36) or approx. 900 g (2 lb)
  sugar quantity Royal Icing (page 32)
green liquid food colouring
100 g (4 oz) Fondant Moulding Paste
  (only if using royal icing)
450 g (1 lb) sugar quantity Royal Icing,
  for decoration
approx. 2 metres (6 feet) white or pale
  to mid-green ribbon, 5 mm (¼ inch)
  wide (optional)

Preparation time: icing and
decoration of the cake, plus time for
drying the plaques

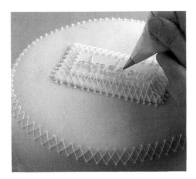

Over-piping the child's name
in a second colour on the
central plaque

Using a No. 3 or 2 writing
nozzle to pipe small birds on
the top of the cake

1. Brush the top and sides of the cake
with apricot glaze and coat with
marzipan. Leave to dry.
2. Stand the cake on the board. Brush
the marzipan with egg white if using
the moulding paste. Tint all but 100 g
(4 oz) of the moulding paste a pale
green by kneading in a little green food
colouring until evenly blended. Roll
out and use to cover the cake smoothly
and evenly. Leave to dry. If using royal
icing, make up and tint it a pale green.
Use it to give the cake 2 coats all over
and a third coat to the top. Leave to
dry.
3. Thinly roll out the reserved
moulding paste or the 100 g (4 oz)
moulding paste if you have used royal
icing for base icing the cake. Cut into
two rectangular plaques: one 11 ×
6 cm (4½ × 2½ inches) and the other 9
× 4 cm (3½ × 2½ inches). Leave to
dry on non-stick silicone paper.
4. Make up the royal icing for
decoration and leave it white. Attach
the larger plaque centrally to the cake
with icing, then put the smaller one
centrally on top of it and attach it with

a little more icing. Write the name of
the child on a piece of paper and prick it
out on the top plaque. Put some white
icing into a piping bag fitted with a No
2 writing nozzle and outline the name.
Leave to dry.
5. Put some white icing into a piping
bag fitted with a No. 1 writing nozzle
and pipe a series of slanting lines all
round the top edge of the smaller
plaque over the larger one and on to the
cake. When dry, pipe a series of lines in
the opposite direction over the first
ones to form a lattice. Leave to dry,
then pipe a small dot at the joins of each
diamond of trellis to neaten it off.
6. Work a similar trellis over the top
edge of the cake. Begin on top of the
cake about 1 cm (⅓ inch) in from the
edge and finish about the same distance
below the edge on the side of the cake.
Leave to dry.
7. Tint a little icing a slightly deeper
shade of green than the base icing and
put into a piping bag fitted with a
No. 2 writing nozzle. Overpipe the
name of the child either in a plain line
or as a series of dots. Next pipe a dot in
the centre of each lattice diamond right
on the top edge of the cake.
8. To make the birds, use a No. 3 or 2
writing nozzle and white icing. On the
top of the cake mark out positions
evenly for the 6 birds to line up with
the central plaque and edge of the cake.
Take the piping bag and pipe a pear-
shaped head facing in to the centre of
the cake for the single birds and facing
towards each other for the pairs. Next,
for the body, pipe a larger 'comma'
shape under the head, with the tip
pointing almost downwards but in the
same direction as the beak. Leave to
dry. For the wing, pipe a smaller
comma shape over the body but with
the tip pointing out in the opposite
direction from the beak.
9. With the No. 2 or 1 writing nozzle
and white icing, pipe a large and small
dot each side of the single birds; 1
larger and 2 smaller dots on the outside
of the pairs of birds and 1 large dot
with a smaller one each side of it in
between them.

10. Repeat the pairs of birds and dots around the sides of the cake.

11. For the base border, pipe a continuous line of dots around the cake to attach it to the board, using the larger of the writing nozzles already used and white icing. Next pipe a dot above and below every other dot and slightly smaller than the first ones on the side of the cake and on the board.

12. If liked, tie narrow ribbon around the cake below the line of birds. Attach with dabs of icing and pins, removing the pins when dry.

Christening Cake with its decoration completed

Birthday
Greetings
Jessica

SQUARE BIRTHDAY CAKE

1 × 20 cm or 23 cm (8 or 9 inch)
    square Rich Fruit Cake (pages 18-19)
1 quantity Apricot Glaze (page 30)
800-900 g (1¾-2 lb) Marzipan (page
    30)
25 or 28 cm (10 or 11 inch) square
    silver cake board
little egg white
900 g-1 kg (2-2½ lb) Fondant
    Moulding Paste (page 36)
approx 50 piped royal icing pink tea
    roses with white or pale green
    centres (page 62)
approx 24 pale green small piped leaves
    (page 62)
225 g (8 oz) sugar quantity Royal Icing
    (page 32)
pink and green liquid food colourings

Preparation time: icing and
decoration of the cake, plus time for
making and drying the flowers, leaves
and frills

1. Cover the cake using the apricot
glaze and marzipan. Stand on the cake
board and leave to dry.
2. Brush the marzipan lightly with egg
white. Use most of the fondant
moulding paste to cover the cake
smoothly and evenly. Leave to dry.
3. Make the pink roses and leaves and
leave to dry.
4. Make a template for the design of
the flowers on top of the cake. Fold a
19 cm (7½ inch) square into a triangle,
fold the triangle in half, then in half
once again. Draw a small curve from
the folded edge, then a deep petal shape
to within about 2 cm (¾ inch) of the
top of the paper. Cut out. Position on
the cake.
5. Tint the royal icing pink to match
the flowers and put into a piping bag
fitted with a small writing nozzle, then
outline the template.
6. Prick out the words 'Birthday
Greetings' and the name of the person
inside the piped line and pipe over with
pink or green icing. Leave to dry, then
overpipe.

7. Arrange the pink flowers and green
leaves over the outlined shape made by
the template, attaching with a dab of
icing.
8. Make a template for the sides of the
cakes. Cut out a strip of paper the
length of the side and two-thirds of the
depth of the side. Fold into quarters
and draw a shallow curve on it. Don't
make this too deeply curved or it will
be difficult later to add the frills so that
they don't break.
9. For the frilling on the side of the
cake, tint the remaining fondant paste
the same pink or a little paler than the
flowers and roll out thinly. Cut into
strips about 2 cm (¾ inch) wide, then
mark a line along the length of each
strip about 5 mm (¼ inch) down from
the top edge. Next, take a wooden
cocktail stick and roll it gently from
side to side below the marked line, to
thin out the icing. This should make
the frilling. Do not attempt to make the
frills too long or they will break as you
try to pick them up.
10. Fit the template round the sides of
the cake and pipe a line of pink icing on
to the side of the cake to follow the
scallop lines. Attach the frilling to this
line. Make joins as and when necessary
by slightly moistening the ends of the
frills, pressing together and rubbing
over the joins with the fingertips. The
frilling must be added while still soft or
it will become brittle and be difficult to
handle.
11. Using a medium writing nozzle
and pink icing, pipe a series of dots all
round the base of the cake to attach it to
the board. Next, pipe another dot
directly under the point of the curved
frill just above the base dot, then a
smaller one still above that. Add a
fourth dot with the fine nozzle. Add 2
dots of graduating sizes above the dots
each side of the central one; and one dot
over the one each side beyond that one.
Repeat under all the points of the frills.
12. Add a pink rose and 2 small leaves
by every other dot decoration on the
board, so that the flower tilts slightly
up the cake but the leaves are on the
board. Leave to dry.

Opposite: the Square Birthday
Cake, pink and pretty with
flowers, is just right for a girl

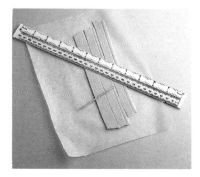

Strips of fondant moulding
paste cut and marked ready to
make the frills for the cake

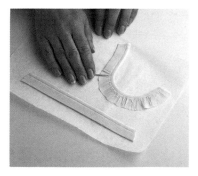

Gently rolling a toothpick
along the strips below the
marked line to 'frill' them

ENGAGEMENT CAKE

Marking out the guide lines on plain card or paper for piping the royal icing fans

Fan patterns piped on to a sheet of non-stick silicone paper over the guide card

Primroses
Mould elongated shapes from balls of pale yellow icing. Make a cut across the top about halfway down, but off centre. Snip into 5 petals. Bend out the petals, working them thin. Cut out a tiny nick from the centre of each petal. Paint in the centre of the flower with a darker colouring.

1 oval Rich Fruit Cake approx 25 × 15 cm (10 × 6 inch) made using quantities for 23 cm (9 inch) square or cut from a 25 cm (10 inch) round cake (pages 18–19)
1 quantity Apricot Glaze (page 30)
approx 800 g (1¾ lb) Marzipan (page 30)
silver cake board approx 5 cm (2 inches) larger than the cake or a rectangular board or a 30 cm (12 inch) round board
little egg white
900 g (2 lb) Fondant Moulding Paste (page 36) or 1.25 kg (2½ lb) sugar quantity Royal Icing (page 32)
green liquid food colouring
For decoration:
about 10 moulded primroses (see left) and 8 moulded snowdrops (page 72)
green leaves (page 62), optional
225 g (8 oz) sugar quantity Royal Icing
3 metres (10 feet) very narrow white ribbon

Preparation time: icing and decoration of cake, plus time for making and drying fans and flowers

1. Cover the cake using the apricot glaze and marzipan. Stand on a cake board and leave to dry.
2. If using fondant paste, brush the marzipan lightly with egg white. Tint the fondant a pale green and use to cover the cake smoothly and evenly. If using royal icing, tint most of it a pale green and use to give 2 coats all over the cake. Leave to dry.
3. Make the flowers and leave to dry.
4. Use the 225 (8 oz) of royal icing to make the fans for decoration. It is wise to make extra as they are very fragile and some will probably break as they are moved and attached. Take a sheet of card and draw a continuous line along the length of it, then draw a second line 1 cm (½ inch) below it broken into short lines of 2 cm (¾ inch) with about 1 cm (½ inch) gap between. Repeat these lines all over the card. These are the basis for the fan

patterns. Using each short line as a base, draw 5 petal shapes as a guide to making the fan. Repeat this 2–3 times (once you have piped 2 or 3 fans no extra guide lines will be necessary). Cover the card with a sheet of non-stick silicone paper, attaching it firmly with drawing pins or sticky tape.
5. Fit a piping bag with a fine writing nozzle (No. 0 or 1) and half fill with royal icing. To pipe the fan shapes, start in the centre of one of the 2 cm (¾ inch) lines, work round the petals, moving up to the tallest central point and back down again the other side, keeping to the 2 cm (¾ inch) line for length and to the continuous line to give the height. You will need at least 18 fans to go round the top of the cake and at least 28 for round the base. Leave to dry in a warm place. If you can't get them all on one sheet, make another in the same way.
6. Mark the top edge of the cake with a pin at 2 cm (¾ inch) intervals, to match the width of the fans. With the writing nozzle and white icing, pipe a series of loops between these marks. When dry, pipe a second line of loops all round to fit in between each of the first loops. Leave to dry.
7. Prick out the words 'Good Luck' on top of the cake and write over it using the same nozzle and a double row of piping. Leave to dry, then overpipe.
8. Fill a piping bag fitted with a medium writing nozzle (No. 3) with white icing and pipe a border of dots all round the base of the cake keeping them even-sized, then pipe a smaller dot above every third dot. Take the smaller writing nozzle and pipe a yet smaller dot on top of the previous 2.
9. Pipe a series of loops from the top dot to the next top dot all the way round the cake.
10. Using a pair of tweezers, attach the fans carefully to the top of the cake with a tiny dab of icing, so that each stands up between alternate loops. Pipe a small dot at the top of the loop joins between the fans to finish it off.
11. Attach fans all the way round the base of the cake, sticking them so they

point outwards and stand upright. Position them between each third large dot, in the middle of and below each loop. Leave to dry.

12. Tie 2 or 3 narrow ribbons around the sides of the cake, attaching with

dabs of icing and pins. Remove the pins when the icing is dry.

13. Arrange flowers and leaves (if using) in decorative clusters on top of the cake around the writing, attaching with icing.

The completed Engagement Cake, wishing the happy couple 'Good Luck'

HEXAGONAL WEDDING CAKE

1 × 28 cm (11 inch) and 1 × 18 cm
  (7 inch) round Rich Fruit Cake
  (pages 18-19) or Rich Fruit Cake
  with Sherry (pages 20-1)
1 quantity Apricot Glaze (page 30)
1.6 kg (3½ lb) Marzipan (page 30)
approx 2.9 kg (6½ lb) sugar quantity
  Royal Icing (page 32)
33 cm (13 inch) and 20 cm (8 inch)
  round silver cake boards
mauve liquid food colouring
little egg white or lemon juice
approx. 120 piped fans (page 58)
approx. 40 run-out heart shapes (see
  below)
4 white cake pillars

Preparation time: icing and
decoration of the cake, plus time for
making and drying the fans and hearts

Piping a small quantity of
icing on to the hearts to attach
them to the cake

Using a pair of tweezers to
attach the fans carefully to the
cake

If you can hire or borrow hexagonal-
shaped tins, bake the cakes in sizes of 25
and 15 cm (10 and 6 inch); if not, make
the slightly larger sizes and cut out as
described on page 9.
1. Brush the tops and sides of the cakes
with apricot glaze and coat with
marzipan. Leave to dry.
2. Make up some of the royal icing and
attach each cake to the appropriate
board with a dab of icing. Flat ice the
cakes giving 3 coats all over and a
fourth to the tops, if necessary. Leave
to dry.
3. Tint a little of the icing a pale mauve
with the food colouring and put into a
piping bag fitted with a fine writing
nozzle (No. 1 or 0). Make
approximately 120 fans as for the
Engagement Cake (page 58) with bases
of 2 cm (¾ inch). Leave to dry.
4. For the run-out hearts, draw a heart
shape, which fits into a 2.5 cm (1 inch)
square, all over a sheet of card or stiff
paper. Cover with a sheet of non-stick
silicone paper and using a No. 1 or 2
writing nozzle and mauve icing,
outline at least 40 heart shapes. Leave to
dry. For 10 of the hearts, work a lattice
pattern to fill the shapes. For the

others, thin a little mauve icing with
egg white or lemon juice until it flows,
then put into a greaseproof paper icing
bag without a nozzle. Cut off the tip
and use to flood the hearts. Prick any
air bubbles and leave to dry.
5. Make up the rest of the icing as and
when necessary. Take a piping bag
fitted with a No. 1 writing nozzle and
white icing and pipe a series of dots all
round the run-out hearts just in from
the edge (but not on the lattice ones).
6. On the large cake at the base, mark
each section into 4 by putting small
dabs of icing as markers. Divide the
small cake into 3 sections similarly. Fill
a piping bag fitted with a medium star
nozzle and white icing and pipe twisted
scrolls in a clockwise movement,
graduated in size from small to large
and back to small again, all around the
base of both cakes to fill in between the
markers. Leave to dry.
7. Attach 3 hearts (2 run-outs and one
lattice) centrally to each side of the
large cake and 2 hearts (both run-outs)
on the small cake. Use just a small cab
of icing to attach each one.
8. For the top of the large cake, prick
out a line 6 cm (2¼ inches) long and
2.5 cm (1 inch) in from the edge of the
cake on each section. Attach 3 fans to
each of these lines with icing, so that
they stand up.
9. For the smaller cake, prick a line
4 cm (1½ inches) long and again
2.5 cm (1 inch) in from the edge.
Attach 2 fans to each line in the same
way and leave to dry.
10. Take a piping bag fitted with a No.
2 or 3 writing nozzle and filled with
white icing and pipe 3 dots centrally
inside the fans on top of the cake, as in
the picture. Next pipe one centrally on
the outer side of the fans with a slightly
smaller one each side of it. Finally take
a No. 1 writing nozzle and white icing
and complete the central design by
piping 4 graduated dots towards the
centre of the cake from the middle dot,
and 2 graduated dots from the outer
ones. On the outer side of the fan, pipe
3 more graduated dots to reach the end
of the fans. On the smaller cake fewer

The completed Hexagonal Wedding Cake assembled for the great day

dots will be required to fit in with only 2 fans, but keep to the same general pattern.

11. Attach fans all around the top edge of the cakes, facing outwards. You need 7 for each section on the large cake and 5 for the smaller cake.

12. Take the No. 1 writing nozzle and white icing and pipe a large dot at the bottom and in the middle of each fan on the top of the cake with a smaller

one on each side. Do the same under the fans on the side of the cake.

13. Finally, using the same nozzle, pipe a squiggly white line of icing along the top of each scroll at the base of the cakes and attach a fan at each corner. Leave to dry.

14. Assemble the cake, placing the smaller tier evenly on top with the sides matching. Top the cake with a vase of small white or mauve flowers.

Purchased decorations
Elaborate decorations which may be bought include: coloured butterflies made of wire and coloured netting; fragile gum paste leaves, of various designs, set in moulds and backed with net; birds of varying sizes and types available in plastic and plaster; horseshoes, leaves, hearts, bows, shoes and cupids in many shapes and sizes, in silver, gold and white; and varying widths of silver and gold paper banding.

Piped roses Fill a piping bag fitted with a petal nozzle with white royal icing. Attach a small square of non-stick silicone paper to an icing nail or cork impaled on a skewer with a dab of icing.

Hold the icing bag so that the thin edge of the nozzle is pointing upwards, then, squeezing evenly and twisting the nail at the same time, pipe a tight coil for the centre of the rose. Continue to add 5 or 6 petals, piping the icing and twisting at the same time, but taking each petal only about three-quarters of the way round the flower. Begin in a different part of the flower each time and make sure the base of the nozzle tips in towards the centre of the flower or the rose will expand at the base and the top instead of just at the top.

For rose buds, keep the petals tight and only add 2 after the first central coil has been piped.

Piped leaves Use a special leaf nozzle and white royal icing. Attach a square of silicone paper to an icing nail.

Begin with the nozzle touching the paper and the end turned up a fraction. Press gently and as the icing begins to emerge, raise the nozzle slightly. When the leaf is large enough break off sharply to leave a point. The bag can be gently twisted or moved up and down to give different shapes, the size can be increased by extra pressure. Leave to dry.

SQUARE WEDDING CAKE

1 × 15 cm (6 inch), 1 × 20 cm (8 inch) and 1 × 25 cm (10 inch) square Rich Fruit Cake (pages 18-19) or Rich Fruit Cake with Sherry (pages 20-1)
2 quantities Apricot Glaze (page 30)
2.3 kg (5 lb) Marzipan (page 30)
3.5-4 kg (8-9 lb) sugar quantity Royal Icing (page 32)
blue liquid food colouring
20 cm (8 inch), 25 cm (10 inch) and 33 cm (13 inch) square silver cake boards
24 white doves (see right)
24 piped white roses (see left)
24 piped white rose buds (see left)
24 piped white leaves (see left)
7 or 8 white square pillars

Preparation time: icing and decoration of the cake, plus time for making and drying the doves, roses and leaves

1. Brush the tops and sides of the cakes with apricot glaze and coat with marzipan. Leave to dry.
2. Make up some of the royal icing and tint it a pale to mid-blue with the food colouring. Use a little to attach the cakes to the appropriate boards. Flat ice the cakes, giving each cake 3 coats all over and a further coat to the tops of the cakes, especially the large one, if necessary. Leave to dry.
3. Make the doves and leave to dry.
4. Make the roses, buds and leaves and leave to dry.
5. Draw a template for the top of the cake (as in the photograph) making the corner square 2.5 cm (1 inch) on the top tier; 4 cm (1½ inches) for the middle tier and 5 cm (2 inches) for the base tier. Position the templates on the cakes.
6. For the sides of the cake make corner templates which are the same width as the square in the corner but, halfway down the side of the cake, they slant out, so that they are one inch wider when they reach the board. Position on the cake.

7. Make up some more of the royal icing, leaving it white. Fit a piping bag with a No. 1 writing nozzle, fill with white icing and outline first the square corners, taking the icing from the point of each square on the top of the cake down the sides to the base. Next outline the curved part of the template on top of the cakes. Remove the templates and leave the piped outlines to dry.
8. On the board mark a line from the edge of the side outline to the corners of the boards and outline in icing, then mark a double loop on the board between the 2 corner outlines and outline with icing.
9. Pipe a second line of piping on the side of the curves on top of the cake nearest the edge of the cake, then pipe 2 more lines inside the corner shapes, taking the line down inside the whole shape over the sides and cake board. Leave to dry, then overpipe the central line.
10. Fill the outlined corner shapes with very fine lacework (see page 11) using a No. 1 or 0 writing nozzle and white icing, on all of the cakes.
11. Using a No. 3 writing nozzle and white icing, pipe a twisted looped border to the top of the cake in between the lacework panels; and another one at the base to attach the cake to the board. Next, with the fine writing nozzle, pipe a narrow scalloped line just under the top edge border on the side of the cake.
12. Attach a dove at the central point of each loop on top of the cakes and another one at each corner of the cake on the board with the tails facing outwards.
13. On the large cake attach 3 roses, 2 buds and 2 leaves on the sides of the cake, centrally between the lacework panels; on the middle tier add 2 roses, 2 buds and 2 leaves; and on the small cake add 1 rose, 2 buds and 2 leaves, attaching all with a dab of icing. Assemble the cake tiers, using 4 pillars on the bottom and 3 or 4 on the middle tier. Place an arrangement of flowers on the top.

To make doves
On non-stick silicone or waxed paper draw pairs of opposite right angles with lines 1.5 cm (½ inch) long. These are for the wings. Using white royal icing and a No. 1 writing nozzle, begin inside one of the right angles, pipe up the vertical line, then continue from this point in a curve down to the end of the horizontal line (to make almost a petal shape but in fact a feather) and return to the top of the vertical line. Fill in the rest of the wing with more curved 'feathers' each decreasing in size until you have 5 feathers, all just touching.

For the tail, pipe first a dot, then 2 straight feathers extending outwards from this dot, a similar shape to the wings, with the lower one slightly longer than the other.

For the body, use a No. 2 writing nozzle and pipe out a row of 'bulbs' of white icing by starting at the tail end and piping 6 continuous bulbs without taking the nozzle off the shape and finishing the head off with a sharp movement to give a 'beak'. Leave all to dry.

To assemble, attach the wings to the body with a small dab of icing, making sure you have the ridged edge upwards, then attach the tail. Leave again to dry. Take great care when moving the doves, for they are very fragile, and make extra, especially of the wings and tails.

THREE-TIER ROUND WEDDING CAKE

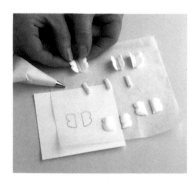

Butterflies Draw the butterfly wings separately on a piece of stiff card, tracing from a picture if you can't manage freehand. Place a piece of non-stick silicone paper over the drawing and attach it, so that it is flat. Using a writing nozzle and white icing, outline the wings. Thin a little royal icing with the lemon juice or egg white until it just flows. Put into a paper icing bag without a nozzle, cut off the tip and pipe into the outline until it is filled. Prick any air bubbles and leave to dry. Repeat by moving the non-stick silicone paper over the pattern. Outline the wings in pale pink icing using a fine writing nozzle (No. 0) and pipe a little lacework over them. Leave to dry. To assemble: use pink icing and a No. 2 writing nozzle to pipe a squiggle the length of the wings. Press on a pair of wings, one each side of the body, and leave to set.

1 × 12.5 cm (5 inch) round, 1 × 20 cm (8 inch) round and 1 × 28 cm (11 inch) round Rich Fruit Cake (pages 18-19) or Rich Fruit Cake with Sherry (pages 20-1)
2 quantities Apricot Glaze (page 30)
2 kg (4½ lb) Marzipan (page 30)
3.5-4 kg (8-9 lb) sugar quantity Royal Icing (page 32)
round silver cake boards 18 cm (7 inch), 25 cm (10 inch) and 35 cm (14 inch)
pink and green liquid food colourings
about 120 daisies with pink centres
about 25 white and pink butterflies
7 or 8 white cake pillars

Preparation time: icing and decoration of the cake, plus making and drying the daisies and butterflies

1. Brush the tops and sides of the cakes with apricot glaze and coat with marzipan (see page 31). Leave to dry.
2. Make up some of the royal icing and attach each cake to the appropriate board with a dab of icing. Flat ice the cakes giving 3 coats all over and a further coat to the tops of the cakes, especially the large one (see pages 33-4). Leave to dry for 24 hours.
3. Make the daisies and butterflies (see left) and allow to dry.
4. Draw 3 circles on thin card 2.5 cm (1 inch) smaller than the top of each of the cakes for templates and cut out. Fold each into eighths, then draw a deep petal from the folded edge and shallow curve shape (see page 13).
5. Place the templates centrally on each cake. Place the white royal icing into a piping bag fitted with a fine writing nozzle (No. 1) and use to outline the templates. Remove templates and pipe 2 further lines one inside and one outside the first. Leave to dry. (Keep the piping bag in a polythene bag for later use, see paragraph 7.)
6. Make a template for the sides of each cake. Take a strip of paper the depth and circumference of the iced cake and fold into quarters, then in half again. Draw a shallow curve, then a deep curve to the folded edge keeping to about half the depth of the cake. Cut out, open up and place around the cake to correspond with the top design.
7. Using the white icing, pipe just inside the pattern using the writing nozzle, remove the template and pipe 2 further lines below the first.
8. To make the template for the cake boards, cut a circle the size of each board, then cut off 1 cm (½ inch) all round. Cut out a circle the size of each cake and discard. Fold the remaining rings into quarters, then eighths and draw a petal shape to correspond with that on the sides of the cakes but shallower. Cut out, make one cut into the template and place around the cake on the board. Outline with white icing, leave to dry and remove the template.
9. Tint a little icing pink, or pale forest green if preferred, and put into a piping bag fitted with a No. 1 nozzle. Use to overpipe all the centre outlines on the tops and sides of the cakes.
10. For the lacework, fill a piping bag fitted with a No. 0 nozzle with white icing. Work the lacework pattern (see page 11) to fill the spaces between the icing outlines on the tops and sides of the cakes and between the icing outline and base of the cakes. Leave to dry.
11. For the base border, fill a piping bag fitted with a large writing nozzle (No. 3 or 4) with white icing and pipe a border of plain large dots all round the base of the cakes to attach to the board.
12. To complete the decoration, on the small cake add 1 daisy (see below) to each point of the shallow curve on top of the cake, 1 at the join of deep curves on the sides and 1 centrally opposite the deepest part of each curve on the board, attaching each with a dab of icing. Add 2 daisies in each matching place on the middle tier and 3 daisies on the large tier. Attach 1 butterfly (on each tier) on the top edge of the cake at the points of the curves and where the lacework joins the cake on the base. Leave to dry.
13. Assemble the cake and put a small arrangement of flowers on the top tier.

A delicate arrangement of flowers tops the assembled Three-Tier Round Wedding Cake

Daisies

Using white royal icing, fill a piping bag fitted with a medium petal nozzle and attach a small square of non-stick silicone paper to an icing nail with icing. Pipe 6 pointed petals keeping the thickest end of the nozzle to the centre and the piping bag upright, with all the centres touching. Leave to dry.

Tint a little icing a pale pink to match the cake and put into a piping bag fitted with a No. 1 or 2 writing nozzle. Pipe a dot in the centre of each flower and leave to dry.

AMERICAN WEDDING CAKE

1 × 15 cm (6 inch) round, 1 × 20 cm
  (8 inch) round and 1 × 25 cm
  (10 inch) round Rich Fruit Cake
  (pages 18-19) or Rich Fruit Cake
  with Sherry (pages 20-1)
2 quantities Apricot Glaze (page 30)
1.75 kg (4 lb) Marzipan (page 30)
approx 2.75 kg (6 lb) sugar quantity
  Royal Icing (page 32)
33 cm (13 inch) thick round silver cake
  board
23 cm (9 inch) and 18 cm (7 inch)
  medium thick or thin but extra firm
  cake boards (silver)
cream and golden yellow liquid food
  colourings
approx 50 white moulded roses of
  varying sizes (see right)
approx 60 cream moulded roses of
  varying sizes
approx 60 pale golden yellow moulded
  roses of varying sizes
approx 30 purchased silver or white
  moulded leaves

Preparation time: icing and
decoration of the cake, plus making
and drying of the roses

Do not add any glycerine to the icing
which you use for the 4 coats on top of
the base cake. It has to be hard enough
to take the weight of the other 2 cakes.
1. Brush the tops and sides of the cakes
with apricot glaze and coat with
marzipan. Leave to dry.
2. Make up some of the royal icing and
attach each cake to the appropriate
board with a dab of icing. Flat ice the
cakes, giving 3 coats all over and a
further coat to the top of the base coat.
Leave to dry completely.
3. Make the roses, using about 450 g
(1 lb) fondant moulding paste (see
right), and leave to dry. Also make the
leaves if using moulded ones.
4. On the tops of the base and middle
cakes, mark the size of the boards
which will stand on them (for the next
cake up) with pin pricks or dabs of
icing.

5. Draw some scroll shapes or paper to
fit around the top space outside the
cake boards on the middle and bottom
tiers, the one for the base being rather
more elongated. Place these at 4 equal
points on each cake and prick out.
6. Make up the rest of the royal icing
as necessary. Fill a piping bag fitted
with a No. 2 writing nozzle with white
icing and outline the scrolls, then pipe a
second scroll shape beside the first
piping. Leave to dry, then overpipe one
line of the scrolls.
7. For the sides of all the cakes, draw
vertical scroll shapes which work as a
mirror-image pair. Prick these shapes
on to the sides of the cakes.
8. Using the writing nozzle, pipe
double lines in white icing as for the
first scrolls, dry, then overpipe one
with white icing. Leave to dry.
9. Fit a piping bag with a medium star
nozzle and fill with white icing. Pipe a
fairly heavy shell border around the top
edge of the 3 cakes. Leave to dry.
10. Fill a piping bag fitted with a fine
writing nozzle (No. 1 or 0) and pale
gold icing and pipe a continuous
slightly looped line to fit around the
shells both on top of the cake and on
the sides. Leave to dry.
11. To assemble the cakes, stand the
base on something flat, then put the
middle tier carefully on top, so that the
scrolls correspond.
12. Work a white shell border as on the
top edges of the cakes to attach the base
cake to the board and middle tier to the
base cake. Do the same to the top tier.
13. With the fine writing nozzle and
gold icing, pipe a slightly scalloped line
above and below the shell borders as on
the tops of the cakes.
14. Starting on top of the cake, arrange
a cluster of roses of varying colours and
sizes, attaching with dabs of icing.
Continue in a heavy swirling cascade of
roses down the sides and over the tops
of each of the cakes to the base. Keep
the colours mixed and fill in the gaps
with leaves. On each of the tiers, mid-
way between the scrolls on the sides of
the cake, attach one rose and three rose
buds. Allow to dry completely.

Using royal icing to pipe a
shell border to attach the top
to the middle tier of the
American Wedding Cake

Moulded roses
These are made in the
same way as marzipan
roses (see page 51), but
they can be made simply
by taking small scraps of
paste and pressing them
out thinly into circles
between thumb and
finger rather than rolling
out and cutting the
circles. Make some buds
using just 2 circles of
icing, make the flowers
with 3 or 4 petals and
some quite large ones
with 5 or so petals. Leave
on non-stick silicone
paper for about 48 hours
in a warm place to dry.
They may be made some
time in advance. Once
completely dry moulded
roses will store
satisfactorily for several
months before use.

GOLDEN WEDDING CAKE

1 × 25 × 15 cm (10 × 6 inch) rectangular Rich Fruit Cake (pages 18-19) or a 25 cm (10 inch) square cake trimmed to the correct size
1 quantity Apricot Glaze (page 30)
900 g (2 lb) Marzipan (page 30)
approx. 2.25 kg (4 lb) sugar quantity Royal Icing (page 32)
30 cm (12 inch) square gold cake board
little egg white or lemon juice
100 g (4 oz) Fondant Moulding Paste (page 36)
gold balls
approx 1 metre (3 feet) narrow gold ribbon (optional)

Preparation time: icing and decoration of the cake, plus making and drying of the collars, plaque, numbers and fans

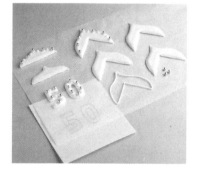

Outlines and filled and decorated outlines for the cake's collars and numbers

Attaching the collars to the corners of the Golden Wedding Cake

1. Brush the top and sides of the cake with apricot glaze and coat with marzipan. Leave to dry.
2. Make up some of the royal icing and use a good dab to attach the cake to the board.
3. Flat ice the cake giving it 2 coats all over and a third coat to the top if necessary. Leave to dry. Make up the rest of the royal icing as needed.
4. Meanwhile make the collars. On a sheet of paper, cut out a corner to fit the corners of the cake exactly. Draw a curved shape as in the picture which measures 4 cm (1½ inches) along each side. Cut this shape out and transfer the shape to a sheet of card. Also draw shapes for the collars for the long sides of the cake, which should be 5 cm (2 inches) long.
5. Lay a sheet of non-stick silicone paper over the collar templates. Using a No. 2 writing nozzle and white icing, outline them, making at least 8 collars for the corners and 4 for the sides to allow for breakages.
6. Next place the paper collar templates around the base of the cake on the board and outline with white icing and the same writing nozzle.

7. Draw a 5 and a 0 on the card, cover with the silicone or waxed paper and outline, making 3 of each, again to allow for breakages. (You only need one of each for the cake.)
8. Thin a little of the icing with egg white or lemon juice and put into a greaseproof paper icing bag without a nozzle. Cut off the tip and use to flood the collars and numbers. Prick any air bubbles that come to the surface and leave undisturbed until quite dry.
9. At the same time flood the collar shapes on the cake board, prick air bubbles and leave to dry.
10. Roll out the fondant moulding paste thinly on non-stick silicone paper and trim evenly to a rectangle of approximately 12.5 × 5 cm (5 × 2 inches). Leave to dry completely.
11. To make the fans, using white icing and a No. 1 or 0 writing nozzle, follow the directions for fans on the Engagement Cake (page 58) but make the shape different by piping 4 shallow loops for the first row; 3 loops for the second row; 2 loops for the third and one to complete it, keeping the basic pattern the same size and shape. Make at least 40 fans to allow for breakages. Leave to dry.
12. When the collars are dry, carefully pipe a series of dots all around the outer edge using the fine writing nozzle and add gold balls to every other dot. When dry, attach the collars carefully to the corners and sides of the cake with icing and stand something underneath them to hold in position while they dry.
13. Pipe dots around the collars on the board again adding gold balls to every alternate dot. Do the same to the 5 and 0, adding gold balls to every alternate dot.
14. Using the medium writing nozzle, pipe 'Happy Anniversary' on the plaque. When dry, overpipe. Leave to dry completely, then attach the plaque centrally to the cake with icing.
15. Stand up the 50 at the back of the plaque and attach with icing, holding it in position until dry.
16. On a piece of paper, draw a semi-circle a little wider than the side collar

on the board and prick it out on the side of the cake. Take a piping bag fitted with a No. 2 writing nozzle and pipe a series of dots to outline this shape. Also pipe a series of dots all around the plaque on top of the cake, adding a few gold balls if liked.

17. Using a piping bag fitted with a No. 3 writing nozzle, pipe a border of dots all round the base of the cake except over the run-outs. Next pipe a series of small dots just each side of the outlined semi-circle above 3 alternate dots, with 2 graduated ones each side and 3 in the centre. Pipe another series of dots centrally on the short sides of the cake.

18. Pipe a smaller border of dots around the top edge of the cake and a series of 3, 4, and 3 graduated dots on the long sides under 3 alternate main dots between the 2 collars and centrally on the short sides of the cake.

19. Finally attach 3 icing fans in each corner of the cake as in the picture and 3 by each central collar. Attach 5 fans around each semicircle and one fan at each corner, pointing outwards.

20. Add a small bow of gold ribbon at each corner on top of the cake, if liked.

Marking fifty years of happy marriage: the gold and white Golden Wedding Cake

EIGHTEENTH BIRTHDAY CAKE

1 × 20 or 23 cm (8 or 9 inch) round
   Rich Fruit Cake (pages 18-19)
1 quantity Apricot Glaze (page 30)
800 g (1¾ lb) Marzipan (page 30)
28 cm (11 inch) round silver cake
   board
1.25 kg (2½ lb) sugar quantity Royal
   Icing (page 32) *or* 350 g (12 oz) sugar
   quantity Royal Icing and 900 g (2 lb)
   Fondant Moulding Paste (page 36)
peach liquid food colouring

The Eighteenth Birthday
Cake, celebrating a coming-
of-age

Preparation time: icing and
decoration of the cake, plus time for
drying the run out numbers

1. Cover the cake, using the apricot
glaze and marzipan. Stand on a cake
board and leave to dry.
2. Tint the royal icing a pale peach and
use to give 2 coats all over the cake; *or*
tint the moulding paste pale peach and
use to cover the cake. Leave to dry.
3. Draw the number '18' eight times
on a piece of card, cover with non-stick
silicone or waxed paper and run out the

figures. To do this, tint all the remaining icing a deeper shade of peach and put some into a piping bag fitted with a No. 0 or 1 fine writing nozzle. Outline the figures carefully. Next, thin a little of the icing with lemon juice or egg white, fit into a paper icing bag, snip off the end and use to flood the figures (see picture, top right). Leave the numbers undisturbed to dry completely.

4. Make a template for the cake (see page 13). Draw a 19 cm (7½ inch) circle on thickish paper and cut out. Fold in half and draw a pencil line across the length of the semicircle 2 cm (¾ inch) up from the edge on each side. Next, fold the paper evenly to give 3 even portions. Open out and make a mark 1 cm (½ inch) each side of the folded line at the curved edge. Number these 1 to 4 working from left to right. Draw lines from points 1 and 4 to where the folds meet the pencilled line. Next mark the centre of the pencilled line and draw 2 lines from here to the curved edge to join points 2 and 3. Repeat on the other side. Position on the cake and prick out these shapes with a pin.

5. Using the writing nozzle, pipe out the name in the centre of the cake in the space between the pricked-out shapes. Leave to dry, then overpipe. When dry again, decorate the letters with a series of tiny dots, if liked.

6. Pipe 2 long lines under and above the name, making the one nearest the writing about 2.5 cm (1 inch) shorter at each end.

7. Using the finest writing nozzle you have, work a 5-row trellis to fill the shapes pricked out on top of the cake. To do this, first pipe a series of parallel lines beginning with the 2 outer shapes and keeping in line with the lines already piped on top of the cake, just over 5 mm (¼ inch) apart. For the central shape outline it, then pipe lines parallel with the lefthand side. Turn the cake round and work the remaining 3 shapes in the same way.

8. Turn the cake back again and when the first piping is dry, pipe lines parallel

to the other side of the shape, again keeping equidistant apart. Complete all the trellis in the same way. When dry continue to work the trellis up until you have 5 rows. If you find it very difficult to keep it neat and even, stop after completing 3 layers.

9. For the top edge border begin by fitting a small writing nozzle into a piping bag and fill with deep peach icing. Pipe a series of small dots all around the top edge at about 2 cm (¾ inch) intervals. Then pipe a loop from each of these dots.

10. Pipe a second row of small dots all around in between the first ones. Again work a row of loops from each dot, with slightly deeper curves than the first ones.

11. For the curtain decoration base, first make a template for the curves. Cut a strip of stiff paper about 2 cm (¾ inch) deep. Fold into 4 cm (1½ inch) widths and cut out shallow curves. Open out the strip and place around the sides of the cake, so that it touches the board. Using the writing nozzle, pipe a series of almost touching tiny dots all round to outline the curves. Remove the template and with a medium writing nozzle, pipe a border of dots all round the cake to attach it to the board. Next with the small writing nozzle, pipe a series of dots all round the cake board about 1 cm (½ inch) from the end of the dots, matching one for one with those on the side of the cake.

12. With the fine writing nozzle, work straight lines from the dots on the cake to the corresponding dots on the board keeping it very neat and even. Leave to dry.

13. Attach either six or eight number 18s evenly all round the sides of the cake with tiny dabs of icing. Leave to dry.

The stages in making the run-out '18's for the Eighteenth Birthday Cake

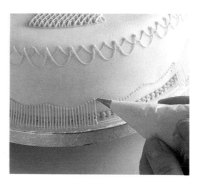

Piping straight lines, or 'curtainwork', from the dots on the side of the cake to the dots on the cake board

Violets These have 4 or 5 mauve petals, each shaped from a circle: 4 are similar in shape, 1 is slightly larger. Press the edges of the circle to thin them. Mould the first circle into an open cone shape. Add 3 similar-sized petals round the top of the flower, pressing the bases together, then place the largest petal under the other 3. Make 4 stamens from yellow icing.

Fuchsias Each flower is made from 2 colours and each has a yellow or green stamen. Make the stamen then, using the first petal colour, cut out 4 petals with a slightly rounded top and elongated base. Gently mould the edge of the top of each, so it is not a sharp cut, then wind these round the stamen. Next cut out 4 sharp-pointed petals from the contrasting colour. Arrange these round the first circle of petals, attaching one at a time to give an open flower.

FLOWER GARDEN CAKE

1 × 20 cm (8 inch) square Rich Fruit Cake (pages 18-19), Rich Fruit Cake with Sherry (pages 20-1) or Madeira Cake (pages 26-7)
1 quantity Apricot Glaze (page 30)
800 g (1¾ lb) Marzipan (page 30)
25 cm (10 inch) square silver or gold cake board
little egg white
800 g (1¾ lb) Fondant Moulding Paste (page 36)
yellow and peach or pink liquid food colourings
225 g (8 oz) sugar quantity Royal Icing (page 32)
selection of moulded flowers – about 60-80 (see below) made from about 450 g (1 lb) fondant moulding paste
selection of green leaves made from about 100 g (4 oz) marzipan or fondant moulding paste

Preparation time: icing and decoration of the cake, plus time for making and drying the flowers and leaves

1. Cover the cake with the apricot glaze and marzipan (see page 31). Stand on a cake board and leave to dry.
2. Brush the marzipan lightly with egg white. Tint the fondant paste a cream colour by kneading in a touch of yellow and either peach or pink food colourings until evenly blended. Use to cover the cake smoothly and evenly (see page 37). Leave to dry.
3. Make the flowers and leaves (see below), put on to non-stick silicone paper and leave to dry in a warm place.
4. Make up the royal icing and tint it to the same shade as the base icing of the cake. Arrange garlands of mixed flowers over the corners of the cake, taking them down to a point in the centre of each side of the cake on the board, attaching with icing. Add a pillar of flowers and leaves at each corner of the cake and attach in the same way. Finally arrange a display on top of the cake in the centre and attach with icing.

5. Fill a piping bag fitted with a medium star nozzle with the cream royal icing and pipe a base border of elongated stars. To do this start on the board, take the nozzle a little way up the side of the cake, then bring back to the board and finish off sharply on the board in a star shape. Leave to dry.

Making Moulded Flowers
Use liquid and/or paste or powder food colourings. Mix small amounts of the appropriate colours into moulding icing (or marzipan if you prefer) until smooth and evenly distributed.
Roses (see page 51) These may be made in any colour you like, provided it is a possible rose colour.
Snowdrops Each flower requires 5 small white oval petals. Shape the first round a cocktail stick and the second petal overlapping this on both sides. Withdraw the stick and mould the other 3 petals round the 'centre' of the flower. Cover the base with a little pale green moulding icing and make a short stem. Leave to dry.
Primroses (see page 58) These should be made in the traditional pale primrose yellow.

CHRISTMAS CAKE WITH ANGELS

1 × 20 cm (8 inch) square Rich Fruit
    Cake (pages 18-19) or Rich Fruit
    Cake with Sherry (pages 20-1)
1 quantity Apricot Glaze (page 30)
33 × 18 cm (13 × 7 inch) silver cake
    board or piece of thick card covered
    with kitchen foil
900 g (2 lb) Marzipan (page 30)
little egg white

approx 900 g (2 lb) Fondant Moulding
    Paste (page 36)
450 g (1 lb) sugar quantity Royal Icing
    (page 32)
yellow and blue liquid food colourings
little lemon juice (optional)
90 piped snowflakes (see below)
14 run-out angels (see below)

Preparation time: icing and
decoration of the cake, plus making
and drying the angels and snowflakes

Departing from the
traditional: the blue and
yellow Christmas Cake with
Angels

1. Cut the cake in half, then cut one piece in half crossways to give 2 small squares. Stand the larger strip of cake on the cake board, brush one short end with apricot glaze and attach one of the small squares, to give a cake of 30 × 10 cm (12 × 4 inches). (Use the remainder of the cake for tea as it will not be needed here.)

2. Brush the top and sides of the cake with apricot glaze and cover with marzipan. Leave to dry.

3. Brush the marzipan lightly with egg white. Roll out the moulding paste and use to cover the cake smoothly and evenly. Leave to dry.

4. To make the snowflakes, make up the royal icing and, using a No. 1 writing nozzle and white icing, pipe out snowflake designs (they should have 6 sides but the patterns can differ) on non-stick silicone paper. Make about 90 and leave to dry.

5. Make 14 angels (see right) and leave to dry completely.

6. Attach 4 angels with a little icing centrally to the top of the cake in a circle with the heads facing inwards, then attach one more at each end of the top. Next attach one angel on each short side and 3 along each long side, all with their heads pointing in the same direction.

7. Using a No. 1 writing nozzle and white icing, pipe a series of slanting straight lines from the top of the cake over the edge, keeping them about 5 mm (¼ inch) apart. Leave to dry. When dry, pipe over the lines to give a trellis effect, taking them from the top of one line on the cake over 2 slanting lines and attaching to the base of the third one. Continue as evenly as possible all the way round the top edge and leave to dry completely.

8. For the base border, fit a piping bag with a medium star nozzle and pipe alternate stars and elongated stars, which spread on to the cake board. At each corner pipe a very much larger pointed and elongated shape which reaches further up the corner of the cake and down on to the board.

9. Finally attach snowflakes all around the angels on the sides and on top of the cake. Leave to dry.

To make angels

Draw angel shapes approximately 5 cm (2 inches) tall on stiff card. Cover with non-stick silicone or waxed paper, then outline the various parts of the body with a piping bag fitted with a No. 2 writing nozzle and white icing. Fill in the hands. Leave to dry. Tint a little icing pale yellow with food colouring and put into a piping bag fitted with a No. 2 writing nozzle. Fill in the hair with a squiggly pattern and leave to dry.

Tint a little more of the icing pale blue with food colouring, then thin it down with a little egg white or lemon juice and put into a greaseproof paper piping bag without a nozzle. Cut off the tip and use to flood the dress. Leave to dry. Thin a little white icing with egg white or lemon juice and put into a paper piping bag without a nozzle. Cut off the tip and use to flood the face and wings. Leave to dry.

RETIREMENT CAKE

1 × 20 or 23 cm (8 or 9 inch) round
  Rich Fruit Cake (pages 18-19) or
  Rich Fruit Cake with Sherry (pages
  20-1)
1 quantity Apricot Glaze (page 30)
575-800 g (1¼-1¾ lb) Marzipan (page
  30)
1-1.25 kg (2-2½ lb) sugar quantity
  Royal Icing (page 32) or 575-800 g
  (1¼-1½ lb) Fondant Moulding Paste
  (page 36)
blue liquid food colouring
25 or 28 cm (10 or 11 inch) round silver
  cake board
175 g (6 oz) Fondant Moulding Paste
  for scroll
approx 1½ metres (5 feet) blue
  ribbon, approx 1 cm (½ inch) wide
little kitchen foil or silver milk bottle
  top for the seal
approx ¼ metre (10 inches) each blue
  and silver ribbon 2.5 cm (1 inch)
  wide for seal

Preparation time: icing and
decoration of the cake, plus time for
scroll to dry

1. Cover the cake with the apricot
glaze and marzipan (see page 31). Leave
to dry.
2. Either flat ice the cake with some of
the royal icing tinted blue giving it 2
coats all over and attaching to the board
with a dab of icing; or cover smoothly
with pale blue fondant moulding paste
(see page 37). Leave to dry. If using
moulding icing, you will need to make
up 225-450 g (½-1 lb) sugar quantity
of royal icing for the decoration.
3. To make the scroll on top of the
cake, roll out the 175 g (6 oz) amount
of moulding paste, so that it is about
5 mm (¼ inch) thick. Cut it to a
rectangle approximately 18 × 9 cm (7
× 3½ inches). Carefully roll one end
under a little using a greased pencil or
knitting needle as a guide. Roll the
other end upwards using a wooden
spoon handle. Put the scroll on a sheet
of non-stick silicone or waxed paper
and leave to dry completely for at least

Pricking through the template
to make guide lines for piping
the scallop border on the cake

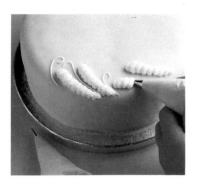

Piped twisted scallops on the
top of the Retirement Cake
made with a medium star
nozzle

48 hours in a warm place until firm.
4. Draw a circle the same size as the
top of the cake and fold into quarters,
then eighths. Open out, place on the
cake and make a small mark on the top
edge of the cake at these points with
icing or a pin. Draw a design on the
paper as in the photograph with lines
down the centre of each of the scrolls.
5. Put the template on the cake and
prick out the various curves with a pin.
These may then be very lightly
scratched in with the point of the pin or
a skewer.
6. Fit a medium star nozzle into a
piping bag and fill with white icing.
Pipe twisted scallops of icing beginning
with the middle of the 3 scrolls in each
group and working from the centre of
the cake out to the edge. Pipe in a
circular movement over and over
clockwise along the scratched or
pricked line but bringing the scroll to
the edge of the cake and tapering off at
the end, whilst gradually releasing the
pressure on the icing bag. Pipe the
outer scrolls next and continue around
the top of the cake. Leave to dry.
7. Using a No. 1 writing nozzle and
white icing, pipe lines over the 2
remaining pricked shapes between the
scrolls on top of the cake.
8. Tie the 1 cm (½ inch) blue ribbon
centrally around the sides of the cake
attaching with a dab of icing and
securing with a pin. Remove the pin
once the icing is dry.
9. Take a piping bag fitted with a No.
1 writing nozzle and white icing and
pipe a scalloped line evenly just above
and just below the ribbon.
10. Using the medium star nozzle,
pipe large shells all around the base of
the cake to attach it to the board. Leave
to dry.
11. Tint some of the royal icing a
deeper shade of blue than the base icing
and put into a piping bag fitted with a
No. 1 or 2 nozzle.
12. Loosen the moulded scroll from
the paper, then, using the deep blue
icing, pipe out the name of the person
who is retiring and the length of service
on the scroll. Leave to dry, then put the

scroll carefully and centrally on the
cake, attaching with icing.
13. For the seal, either mould a piece of
kitchen foil into a seal or use a silver
milk bottle top. Fold pieces of blue and
silver ribbon and attach underneath the
seal with icing. Finally stick the seal on
to the corner of the scroll with icing.

Harry's be-ribboned and
elegantly decorated
Retirement Cake

Continental Gâteaux

Cakes here range from fairly plain recipes to more elaborate gâteaux with many layers and a variety of finishes. They may be served with coffee, tea, as a dinner party dessert, or as part of a celebration buffet. Many of the bases, layers, fillings and toppings can be made in advance, allowing more time to assemble the gâteaux when required.

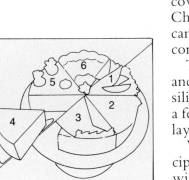

1. A rich topping of marron tuile, orange wedges and chestnut cream
2. Chocolate rose leaves lightly dredged with icing sugar
3. Japonaise wedges, strawberries and crunchy nut topping complete this rich cake
4. Continental butter cream, hazelnut praline and caramel enrich a layered sponge cake
5. Swirls of chocolate icing, topped with marzipan flowers
6. Meringue basket decorated with a sugar-frosted flower

Meringues and japonaise are easier to make if the egg whites are 2-3 days old. They dry out well and do not go sticky. The mixture should be light and marshmallowy. Pipe or spread the meringue or japonaise on to non-stick silicone paper for ease of lifting once they are cooked. Meringues or japonaise may be stored for several weeks in an air-tight tin.

Melted chocolate can produce many different finishes, coatings and decorations. Chocolate may also be melted with milk or cream to produce a smooth, glossy icing for pouring, spreading or, when almost cold, for piping. Chocolate-flavoured cake coverings are acceptable substitutes. Chocolate rose leaves and decorations can be made in advance and stored in a container in a cool place.

Tuille mixture is very fine and light and should be cooked on non-stick silicone paper. Assemble a tuille gâteau a few hours before serving, to allow the layers to soften slightly.

When making the pastry-based recipes, always line the tins or moulds with the pastry and chill thoroughly to prevent shrinkage during cooking. Do not chill pastry cases which are cooked with their filling, but leave them to rest for 30 minutes; otherwise, the base will not cook and the pastry will be soggy.

Torten and light cake mixtures using whisked egg whites are inclined to shrink and dip slightly after cooking, but the texture is light and moist. Fold in $\frac{1}{3}$ of the egg white at a time instead of adding it all at once; this helps keep the volume of mixture more even.

Praline is a versatile recipe; it can be crushed and used as a coating or topping, or for flavouring icings and fillings. Store in a screw-topped jar.

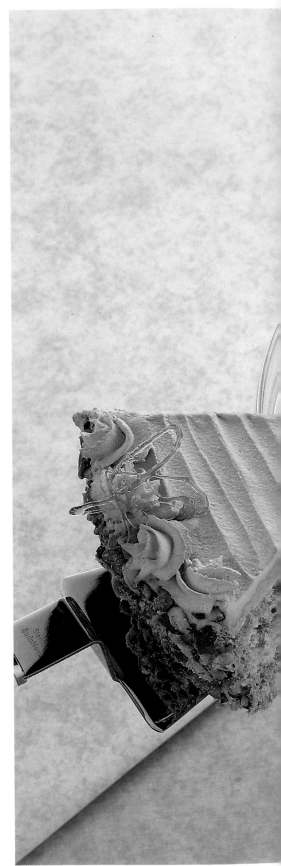

Left: German Torten; right:
Scandinavian Plum Tart

GERMAN TORTEN

Makes one 23 cm (9 inch) round cake
Serves 10-12

Cake:
150 g (5 oz) self-raising flour
50 g (2 oz) ground almonds
100 g (4 oz) caster sugar
5 eggs, separated
3 tablespoons vegetable oil
4 tablespoons boiling water
Chocolate Icing:
100 g (4 oz) plain chocolate
50 g (2 oz) butter
1 egg, beaten
100 g (4 oz) icing sugar
milk (see recipe)
Filling:
450 g (16 oz) marzipan
icing sugar, for dusting
6 tablespoons plum jam, warmed
pink food colouring

Preparation time: 30 minutes, plus
setting
Cooking time: 50-60 minutes
Oven: 180°C, 350°F, Gas
Mark 4

1. Grease and lightly flour a 24 cm
(9½ inch) spring-form tin.
2. Place the flour, ground almonds,
sugar, egg yolks, oil and water in a
bowl. Mix with a wooden spoon, then
beat for 1-2 minutes until smooth.
3. Whisk the egg whites until very stiff
and fold one-third into the mixture,
using a large metal spoon. Add the
remaining egg white and fold in until
the mixture is evenly blended.
4. Pour the mixture into the tin and
bake in the centre of the preheated oven
for 50-60 minutes until well risen and
firm to the touch. Turn out and cool on
a wire tray.
5. To make the chocolate icing, place
the chocolate and butter in a heatproof
bowl over a saucepan of hot water. Stir
occasionally until melted.
6. Stir in the egg and icing sugar, then
heat well until smooth and glossy. Add
a little milk if the icing is too thick to
pour.
7. Lightly dust a board with icing
sugar, roll out a third of the marzipan
thinly and trim into a 20 cm (8 inch)
round, reserving the trimmings.

8. Cut the cake carefully into 4 equal thin layers and place the bottom one on a serving plate.

9. Assemble the cake in layers as follows: Spread the bottom layer with 2 tablespoons of the jam. Spread the second layer with some chocolate icing and place on top of the bottom layer. Cover with the marzipan round, spread with 2 tablespoons jam. Place the third layer on top and spread with some icing. Top with the last layer.

10. Spread the whole cake with the remaining jam, then roll out the remaining marzipan to a round large enough to cover the top and sides of the cake.

11. Carefully place the marzipan over the cake and gently press in position. Trim off any surplus around the base and reserve.

12. Place 1 tablespoon of the remaining icing into a piping bag fitted with a small star nozzle. Warm the remainder, if necessary, then pour over the cake and spread over the top and round the sides with a palette knife. Leave for a few minutes to set.

13. Colour the marzipan trimmings with a few drops of pink food colouring and mould into 12 little flowers (see page 72). Pipe 12 swirls of chocolate icing on top of the cake and place a flower on each.

SCANDINAVIAN PLUM TART

Makes one 24 cm (9½ inch) tart
Serves 6-8

Pastry:
175 g (6 oz) plain flour
25 g (1 oz) caster sugar
125 g (4 oz) butter, cut into pieces
1 egg yolk
cold water to mix
Filling:
40 g (1½ oz) ratafias or macaroons
1 kg (2 lbs) red plums, quartered and
    stoned
6 tablespoons plum jam, warmed
125 ml (¼ pint) whipping cream,
    whipped

Preparation time: 20 minutes
Cooking time: 40-45 minutes
Oven: 180°C, 375°F, Gas Mark 5

1. Place the flour in a bowl, add the butter and rub in finely with the fingers. Stir in the sugar, egg yolk and enough water to mix to a firm dough.

2. Knead on a lightly floured board until smooth. Roll out to a round large enough to line a greased 24 cm (9½ inch) loose-base fluted flan tin.

3. Press pastry into base and flutes, then trim off the surplus with a knife. Prick the base with a fork and chill until firm.

4. Reserve 18 ratafias for decoration, crush the remainder finely and sprinkle evenly over the base of the flan case.

5. Arrange the quartered plums overlapping in circles around the flan case until it is filled and firmly packed.

6. Bake in the centre of a pre-heated oven for 40-45 minutes until the plums are tender and the pastry is pale golden.

7. Leave the flan until cold in the tin, then carefully remove and place on a serving plate.

8. Spoon the plum jam over the plums to cover and glaze evenly.

9. Place the whipped cream in a piping bag fitted with a small star nozzle.

10. When the jam glaze is cold, lightly mark the top of the flan evenly into 6 wedges with a knife.

11. Pipe a zig-zag of cream from the centre to the edge on each marked line, and a swirl of cream in between each. Arrange 2 ratafias at the edge of each cream zig-zag and one at each centre end.

Note
The pastry case for the tart can be made in advance, if time is short, and chilled until ready to fill and use.

If red plums are not available, yellow plums, greengages or apricots make acceptable, pretty-coloured, substitutes in this tart.

Cutting the torten into layers
This cake mixture is light and airy, so when the cake is removed from the oven, the top of the cake will sink slightly as it cools. This does not matter as the cooled cake is to be cut into layers.

When cutting the cake into layers, firstly cut the cake in half, then split each half into 2 layers. The layers are intended to be very thin as the gâteau should be made up of many layers.

TIPSY FRENCH RING

Makes one 23 cm (9 inch) ring cake
Serves 8-10

Cake:
225 g (8 oz) plain flour
1 teaspoon salt
1 teaspoon caster sugar
1½ teaspoons easy blend dry yeast
3 tablespoons warm water
3 eggs
100 g (4 oz) unsalted butter, softened
   and cut into small pieces
Syrup:
175 g (6 oz) sugar
300 ml (½ pint) water
120 ml (4 fl oz) dark rum
Decoration:
2 nectarines, sliced
75 g (3 oz) black grapes, seeded
75 g (3 oz) white grapes, seeded
2 oranges, peeled and segmented
2 tablespoons Apricot Glaze (page 30)
25 g (1 oz) flaked almonds

Preparation time: 35 minutes, plus
                              rising
Cooking time: 20 minutes
Oven: 200°C, 400°F, Gas
                              Mark 6

1. Place the flour, salt, sugar, yeast, water and eggs in a warm bowl. Mix together with a wooden spoon, then beat for 3-4 minutes to form a smooth, elastic batter. (Alternatively, mix in an electric mixer using a dough hook or beater for 1-2 minutes.)
2. Sprinkle the butter pieces over the dough then cover with cling film and leave in a warm place for about an hour, or until the dough has doubled in size.
3. Brush a 23 cm (9 inch) spring-form ring with melted butter and chill until set.
4. Beat the dough with a wooden spoon until all the pieces of butter have been mixed in and the dough is smooth.
5. Carefully spoon the mixture into the ring tin as evenly as possible. Cover the top with cling film and leave in a warm place for about 1 hour, or until the dough has risen almost to the top of the tin.
6. Bake in the centre of the preheated oven for 20 minutes until well risen and golden brown. Remove the ring from the tin and cool on a wire tray.
7. To make the syrup, place the sugar and water in a saucepan and heat gently until the sugar has dissolved. Bring to the boil and boil rapidly for 3 minutes. Allow the syrup to cool, then stir in the rum.
8. Place the ring on a serving plate and pour some of the syrup over. As the ring absorbs the syrup, add some more, and continue in this way until the ring has become saturated with the syrup.
9. Fill the centre with the prepared fruit and arrange any remaining fruit around the base. Brush the ring with apricot glaze and stick flaked almonds around the top.
10. Pour any leftover syrup into a jug and serve with the ring.

FRANZIPAN TART

Serves 8

Pastry:
225 g (8 oz) plain flour
100 g (4 oz) butter, softened and cut
   into pieces
25 g (1 oz) caster sugar
1 egg yolk
about 2 tablespoons cold water
Filling:
4 tablespoons redcurrant jelly
350 g (12 oz) redcurrants
100 g (4 oz) butter, softened
100 g (4 oz) caster sugar
100 g (4 oz) ground almonds
25 g (1 oz) plain flour
few drops almond essence
2 eggs
25 g (1 oz) flaked almonds
1 tablespoon Apricot Glaze (page 30)
whipped cream (optional), to decorate

Preparation time: 20 minutes
Cooking time: 50-60 minutes
Oven: 180°C, 350°F, Gas
                              Mark 4

Preparing fruit
To seed the grapes: make a small slit in the top of each grape. Using a small knife, remove the seeds from the centre of the grapes.

To segment an orange: use a small sharp knife and carefully cut the peel including all the white pith away from the orange flesh. Cut in between the membranes carefully to remove each segment from the orange. Discard the membranes and core.

1. Place the flour in a bowl, add the butter and rub in until the mixture resembles fine breadcrumbs. Stir in the sugar, egg yolk and enough water to mix to a firm dough.

2. Knead on a lightly floured board until smooth. Roll out to a round large enough to line a greased 25 cm (10 inch) loose-bottomed fluted flan tin.

3. Press the pastry on to the base and sides of the tin, then trim off the surplus with a knife. Reserve the trimmings.

4. Prick the base, then spread with the redcurrant jelly. Reserve a few redcurrants for decoration if liked, then distribute the remainder over the jam.

5. Place the butter, sugar, ground almonds, flour, almond essence and eggs in a bowl. Mix together with a wooden spoon, then beat for 1-2 minutes until smooth.

6. Spoon the mixture into the pastry case and level the top.

7. Roll out the pastry trimmings and cut into 5 mm (¼ inch) strips. Arrange them in a lattice design over the filling and trim the edges.

8. Position the flaked almonds on the exposed filling in between the lattice, then bake in a preheated oven for 50-60 minutes until golden brown and firm to the touch. Leave to cool.

9. When cold, brush the top of the tart with apricot glaze and pipe swirls of cream (if using) around the top.

10. Place one of the reserved redcurrants (if using) on each swirl of cream just before serving.

Making pastry lattice
Knead the pastry trimmings together and roll out thinly to a long thin strip about 25 × 10 cm (10 × 4 inch). Cut the pastry into 5mm (¼ inch) strips and place half of the strips across the top of the flan, evenly spaced apart.

Arrange the remaining strips in the opposite direction and press the pastry strips on to the edge of the tin to trim.

Left: Tipsy French Ring; right: Franzipan Tart

GATEAU JAPONAISE

Makes one 20 cm (8 inch) round cake
Serves 8–10

350 g (12 oz) strawberries, hulled and
    sliced
50 g (2 oz) quantity Quick Mix Cake
    mixture (pages 22–3)
Japonaise:
75 g (3 oz) ground almonds
100 g (4 oz) caster sugar
2 egg whites
Decoration:
300 ml (½ pint) double cream
3 tablespoons Kirsch
2 tablespoons crunch nut topping
2 tablespoons strawberry jam
1 teaspoon water

Preparation time: 25 minutes
Cooking time: about 60 minutes
Oven: 160°C, 325°F, Gas
                Mark 3

1. Grease and line a 20 cm (8 inch)
sandwich tin. Stir 100 g (4 oz) of the
strawberries into the cake mixture,
pour into the tin and bake for 20–25
minutes until well risen and firm to the
touch. Turn out to cool on a wire tray.
2. To make the Japonaise, mix the
almonds and 50 g (2 oz) of the sugar
together in a bowl. Whisk the egg
whites until stiff, then whisk the
remaining sugar into them until the
mixture holds soft peaks. Add the
almond mixture and fold in well.
3. Line 2 baking sheets with non-stick
silicone paper and draw a 19 cm
(7½ inch) circle on each. Place the
mixture in a piping bag fitted with a
1 cm (½ inch) plain nozzle. Pipe the
mixture over the circles.
4. Place one baking sheet just above
and one just below the centre of the
preheated oven and bake for 30–35
minutes until lightly browned and firm
to the touch. After 20 minutes remove
one layer and mark it into 12 wedges,
then return it to the oven for another
10–15 minutes.
5. Cool the layers on the paper. Cut
through the wedges on one and remove
the lining paper very carefully.

6. Place the cream and 1 tablespoon of
the Kirsch in a bowl and whip until
stiff. Place one-third in a piping bag
fitted with a small star nozzle.
7. Spread the uncut layer with a layer
of cream, then place the strawberry
cake on top. Spread the sides with
cream and coat evenly with crunch nut
topping. Place on a serving plate.
8. Heat the jam and water together
until melted. Sieve and cool.
9. Spoon the remaining Kirsch over
the top of the cake and spread the
remaining cream evenly over the top.
10. Pipe 10 thin lines of cream
radiating out from the centre and pipe a
shell edging around the top.
11. Position the japonaise wedges in
the cream on top of the gâteau and fill
in between with the remaining
strawberry slices.
12. Brush generously with strawberry
glaze and pipe a swirl of cream in the
centre. Keep cool until ready to serve.

Left: Gâteau Japonaise; right:
Scalloped Fruit Tart

SCALLOPED FRUIT GATEAU

Makes one 23 cm (9 inch) round cake
Serves 8-10

Pastry Case:
200 g (7 oz) plain flour, cut into pieces
150 g (5 oz) unsalted butter, softened
50 g (2 oz) caster sugar
1 egg yolk
Filling:
1 egg white
50 g (2 oz) icing sugar, sieved
50 g (2 oz) flaked almonds, toasted
1 quantity Crème Pâtissière (page 39)
1 red- and 1 green-skinned apple
1 tablespoon lemon juice
4 plums, halved
2 peaches, skinned and sliced
75 g (3 oz) green grapes, seeded
100 g (4 oz) strawberries, hulled
150 ml (¼ pint) tropical fruit juice
1 teaspoon powdered gelatine

Scalloped flan
Form the remaining dough into a short roll and wrap in cling film and chill. Make sure the dough is very firm before slicing it into thin slices, otherwise the roll will go out of shape. To make sure the dough slices fit evenly stand them all around the inside of the tin before pressing them in position. Make sure there are no gaps.

Preparation time: 30 minutes, plus chilling
Cooking time: 40-45 minutes
Oven: 180°C, 350°F, Gas Mark 4

1. Place the flour in a bowl, add butter and rub in until the mixture resembles fine breadcrumbs. Stir in the sugar and egg yolk and mix to a soft dough.
2. Knead on a lightly floured surface until smooth. Roll out half the dough to line the base of a 24 cm (9½ inch) greased spring-form tin.
3. Roll out the remaining dough into a 10 cm (4 inch) long roll and wrap in cling film. Chill the base and the roll until firm.
4. Thinly slice the roll and arrange the slices, overlapping, around the side of the tin. Press the slices together where they overlap and prick the base with a fork.
5. Line the base with greaseproof paper and baking beans. Bake in the preheated oven for 30 minutes, then remove the beans and paper and cook for a further 10-15 minutes, until the pastry is lightly browned and cooked at the base.
6. Leave to cool in the tin, then carefully remove the sides and slide off the base.
7. Whisk the egg white and icing sugar over a saucepan of hot water until stiff. Remove the bowl from the saucepan and whisk until cool to give a stiff meringue. Spread the meringue over the outside of the biscuit case and coat with almonds.
8. Spread the crème pâtissière over the base. Quarter, core and thinly slice the apples and toss in lemon juice. Reserve half of the apple, peach and plum slices, a few strawberry slices and a grape.
9. Combine all the other fruit and scatter over the biscuit base. Arrange the reserved fruits attractively on top. Mix the fruit juice with the gelatine and heat gently until the gelatine has dissolved, then allow to cool.
10. When the fruit juice is beginning to set, spoon over the fruit in the flan case. Leave in a cool place until set.

MARRON TUILE GATEAU

Makes one 20 cm (8 inch) round cake
Serves 8

100 g (4 oz) plain flour
100 g (4 oz) icing sugar, sifted
2 eggs, separated
4 tablespoons milk
1 teaspoon vanilla essence
300 ml (½ pint) double cream
250 g (9 oz) chestnut purée
3 oranges
25 g (1 oz) pistachio nuts, skinned and
  chopped

Preparation time: 20 minutes
Cooking time: 15-20 minutes
Oven: 180°C, 350°F, Gas
                     Mark 4

1. Place the flour, icing sugar, egg yolks, milk and vanilla essence in a bowl. Mix together with a wooden spoon, then beat to form a smooth batter.
2. Whisk the egg whites until stiff, then fold gently but thoroughly into the batter with a large metal spoon.
3. Trace eight 9 cm (3½ inch) circles on a baking sheet lined with non-stick silicone paper. Spread a level tablespoon of the mixture on to each.
4. Bake in the preheated oven for 5 minutes, then quickly loosen each round with a palette knife and return to the oven for 2-3 minutes until golden brown at the edges.
5. Working quickly, roll each round into a cone shape and carefully insert the pointed end of each into a wire tray, so that they will cool standing away from the tray.
6. Line the baking sheet with a fresh piece of non-stick silicone paper and draw three 20 cm (8 inch) circles on it. Spread the remaining mixture over them.
7. Bake for 10-15 minutes until golden brown at the edges. Leave to cool on the paper before removing.
8. Place the cream in a bowl and whip until stiff. Reserve 2 tablespoons, then fold the chestnut purée into the remaining cream.
9. Halve one orange and cut one half into 7 thin wedges. Peel, segment and chop the remaining oranges.
10. Place one tuile layer on a serving plate. Spread with one-quarter of the chestnut cream and half the chopped oranges. Place another tuile layer on top and cover with chestnut cream and oranges as before. Place the remaining tuile layer on top and spread with chestnut cream.
11. Place the remaining chestnut cream in a piping bag fitted with a medium star nozzle. Pipe the cream into each cone and arrange them on top of the gâteau, radiating out from the centre. Add a swirl of chestnut cream in the middle.
12. Use the remaining cream to pipe a swirl at the end of each cone, and one in the centre, and sprinkle a few pistachio nuts over the cream. Arrange orange wedges in between the cones.

AUSTRIAN MERINGUE BASKET

Makes one 20 cm (8 inch) basket
Serves 8-10

Meringue:
6 egg whites
¾ teaspoon cream of tartar
425 g (15 oz) caster sugar
600 ml (1 pint) double or whipping
  cream
3 tablespoons brandy or sherry
40 g (1½ oz) ratafia biscuits, crushed
350 g (12 oz) strawberries, sliced
350 g (12 oz) raspberries
sugar-frosted flowers (page 87) or
  crystallized rose petals

Preparation time: 35 minutes
Cooking time: 1¾-2 hours
Oven: 110°C, 225°F, Gas
                     Mark ¼

1. Line 4 baking sheets with non-stick silicone paper and draw an 18 cm (7 inch) circle on each.

Making tuile cones
Ensure the mixture is spread thinly over each marked circle and cook until the mixture is just beginning to turn a pale golden colour. Remove the baking sheet and loosen each tuile round from the paper, then return to the oven to soften for a few minutes.

Quickly remove only one tuile round at a time and form into a cone shape. If the mixture sets too quickly, return to the oven to soften.

Left: Marron Tuile Gâteau; right: Austrian Meringue Basket

2. Place 4 egg whites and half a teaspoon of cream of tartar into a bowl. Whisk until very stiff, then gradually whisk in 275 g (10 oz) of the sugar. Whisk well after each addition until the meringue is thick and stands in peaks.

3. Place the meringue in a piping bag fitted with a 1 cm (½ inch) plain nozzle. Pipe 2 rings of meringue on the circles on 2 baking sheets and place on the second and third shelves of the preheated oven.

4. Pipe another 2 rings of meringue on the marked circles on the remaining 2 baking sheets, but continue piping to give closed coils, ending in the centre. These will be the basket's lid and base.

5. Pipe a second ring on top of the outer ring of the base layer and place in the oven with the 2 rings. Bake the meringues for 20 minutes, or until firm enough to lift.

6. Loosen the 2 circles from the paper. Pipe a few dots of meringue at intervals around the top edge of the base and place one ring on top. Pipe dots on to the ring and place the second ring on top.

7. Return to the oven with the lid and bake for 20 minutes. Remove the basket and spread the remaining meringue smoothly over the sides. Return to the oven for 20 minutes.

8. Use the remaining egg whites, cream of tartar and sugar to make some more meringue. Place this in a piping bag fitted with a small star nozzle.

9. Remove the basket from the oven and pipe a double row of scrolls around the top and base of the basket. Remove the lid and return to the oven.

10. Pipe the remaining meringue in scrolls around the edge and over the top of the lid. Return to the oven for 45 minutes to 1 hour until the mixture has set. Leave on the paper until cold.

11. Whip the cream and brandy or sherry together until thick. Fold in the ratafias and fruit until evenly blended.

12. Place the basket on a flat serving plate and fill with fruit and cream mixture. Place the lid in position.

13. Use whipped cream to attach sugar-frosted flowers or crystallized rose petals to the side and lid of the basket.

Sugar-frosted flowers
These will only keep for 3-4 days when made but look very pretty on a cake. Use small spring flowers such as violets, primroses, heathers, roses, cherry, apple or pear blossom, and make sure they are unblemished, clean and dry. Lightly beat an egg white, then paint the flower all over with it. Dip twice in caster sugar or scatter the sugar over the flower to coat evenly. Put on non-stick baking parchment and leave in a warm place to dry – about 24 hours. Use at once.

ROSE LEAF GATEAU

Makes one 20 cm (8 inch) round cake
Serves 8–10

Cake:
75 g (3 oz) self-raising flour
25 g (1 oz) cocoa
100 g (4 oz) caster sugar
4 eggs, separated
2 tablespoons vegetable oil
3 tablespoons boiling water

Chocolate Icing:
300 ml (½ pint) double cream
225 g (8 oz) plain chocolate
4 tablespoons black cherry jam,
  warmed
icing sugar, to dredge

Preparation time: 30 minutes, plus
  setting
Cooking time: 45–50 minutes
Oven: 180°C, 350°F, Gas
  Mark 4

Left: Rose Leaf Gâteau; right:
Hazelnut Praline Gâteau

The moule à manque tin has slightly sloping sides which helps the cake to rise but a 20 cm (8 inch) deep cake tin can be used instead.

1. Grease and lightly flour a 20 cm (8 inch) moule à manque tin.
2. Sift the flour and cocoa into a bowl and add the sugar, egg yolks, oil and water. Mix together with a wooden spoon, then beat until smooth.
3. Whisk the egg whites until very stiff and fold one-third into the chocolate mixture using a large metal spoon. Add the remaining egg white and fold in until the mixture is evenly blended.
4. Pour the mixture into the tin and bake in the preheated oven for 45–50 minutes until well risen and firm to touch. Turn out on to a wire tray and cool.
5. To make the chocolate icing, place 150 ml (¼ pint) of the cream and 175 g (6 oz) of the chocolate in a saucepan. Heat very gently, stirring occasionally, until the chocolate has melted.
6. Remove from the heat and cool until the icing is thick enough to coat the back of the spoon. Whip the remaining cream until stiff.

7. Cut the cake into 3 equal layers. Place the bottom one on a wire tray with a plate underneath and spread with half the jam and one-third of the whipped cream.
8. Place the second layer on top and spread with all the remaining jam and half the remaining cream. Cover with the top layer.
9. Pour the chocolate icing over the top of the cake, making sure it runs down the sides, covering them completely. The excess icing should be caught by the plate. Leave the cake for about 30 minutes to set the icing.
10. Mix the chocolate icing on the plate with the remaining whipped cream. Place in a piping bag fitted with a small star nozzle and chill.
11. Melt the remaining chocolate in a heat-proof bowl over a saucepan of hot water, stirring occasionally.
12. Use the chocolate to coat 14 large, 10 medium, 8 small and 5 tiny rose leaves, see box, right.
13. Place the gâteau on a serving plate. Pipe shells of chocolate cream around base. Arrange the rose leaves in circles on top, with the largest leaves outermost. Dredge lightly with icing sugar.

Making chocolate rose leaves
Melt some milk or plain chocolate. Select fresh rose leaves, each on a small stem, and dry thoroughly on kitchen paper. Using a fine paint brush, brush the underside of each rose leaf to cover with a thin layer of chocolate and leave to dry, chocolate side uppermost. Carefully peel the rose leaf away from the chocolate leaf and keep cool until ready to use.

HAZELNUT PRALINE GATEAU

Makes two 20 cm (8 inch) round cakes
Serves 8-9

4 egg quantity Whisked Sponge Cake
  mixture, replacing 25 g (1 oz) plain
  flour with 25 g (1 oz) finely ground
  hazelnuts (pages 24-5)
1 quantity coffee-flavoured
  Continental Butter Cream (page 38)
50 g (2 oz) sugar
2 tablespoons water
50 g (2 oz) hazelnuts, skinned

Preparation time: 35 minutes, plus
  setting
Cooking time: 10-15 minutes
Oven: 180°C, 350°F, Gas
  Mark 4

1. Bake the cake mixture in 2 greased
and base-lined 20 cm (8 inch) sandwich
tins for about 10-15 minutes until well
risen and firm to the touch. Cool on a
wire tray.
2. Place 2 tablespoons of the butter
cream in a piping bag fitted with a
small star nozzle.

3. Cover a board with foil and grease
lightly. Place the sugar and water in a
saucepan and heat gently, stirring
occasionally, until the sugar has
melted. Add the hazelnuts and boil
rapidly until the mixture turns golden
brown.
4. Pour the nuts and nearly all the
caramel on to the foil. Using a
teaspoon, drizzle some of the
remaining caramel into 10-12 abstract
patterns. Leave to set.
5. To make the praline, grind the
cooled nuts and caramel until fine in a
food processor. Split each cake into 2
equal layers.
6. Place the base of one cake on a
serving plate and spread with one-
quarter of the butter cream. Place a
second layer on top and spread with
another quarter of the cream. Place a
third layer on top, spread with another
quarter of the cream, then place the
remaining cake layer on top.
7. Spread the remaining butter cream
over the sides and top of the cake and
press the praline evenly on to the sides.
8. Pipe a scroll edging around the top
of the cake and arrange the caramel
pieces at intervals between the scrolls.

To crush praline
Place the cold nut and
caramel mixture
between 2 sheets of
lightly oiled foil or
greaseproof paper. Tap
firmly with a rolling pin
until evenly crushed.
Place the praline in an
airtight container or
screwtop jar until
required.

Novelty Cakes

These are fun cakes, suitable for any age and most occasions. The basic cake recipes are varied and quick and easy to make. With clever cutting and assembling, they will produce really stunning results. Once each cake has been made, your own personality can show through in the way in which you decorate and finish the cake.

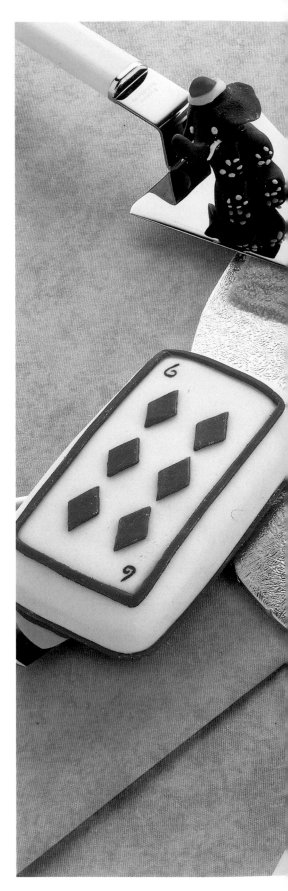

A variety of recipes has been used in this section to produce the different shaped cakes, with the basic Quick Mix Cake, flavoured and coloured, as the basis for many of them. It is baked in a variety of tins and moulds with the minimum amount of trimming needed to obtain the right shape. Whisked sponge mixtures are also trimmed into different shaped cakes, and Swiss rolls are rolled and shaped in unusual ways.

Soft cakes should always be made a few days before they are required, to make cutting and shaping them easier. A coating of apricot glaze over the whole cake, left to set overnight, makes the cake easier to cover with icing.

Butter icings and moulding pastes are the basic coverings for cakes which can be made in advance.

Fondant moulding paste is best used at room temperature; use plenty of icing sugar when rolling it out, and always make sure the icing moves freely on the surface during rolling. When moulding or shaping the paste, use clean hands dipped into cornflour. This helps produce a smooth, glossy surface on a flat-iced cake, and prevents sticking when moulding the icing into flowers, animals or trees.

Moulded items should be made in parts and left almost to set before being assembled. Use egg white to stick the pieces together.

To achieve a smooth surface on butter icing, use a ,small palette knife dipped into hot water to prevent it sticking to the surface.

Always use non-stick silicone paper (or baking parchment) to line baking sheets before cooking the biscuit dough cut-outs, to ensure the shapes lift off easily and cleanly.

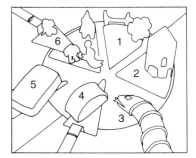

1. A green on the Golf Course novelty cake
2. Sponge cake covered with fondant moulding paste is the basis of this Fairy Castle
3. A lively snake made from a Swiss roll and covered with fondant moulding paste
4. Strips of tinted fondant moulding paste form the colours of the Rainbow cake
5. Playing Card, based on a lemon-flavoured Quick Mix Cake
6. Circus animals and a clown made from fondant moulding paste

SUGAR PLUM FAIRY CASTLE

6-egg quantity Whisked Sponge Cake mixture (pages 24-5)
6 tablespoons Apricot Glaze (page 30)
1½ quantity Fondant Moulding Paste (page 36)
pink food colouring
50 g (2 oz) quantity Quick Mix Cake mixture (pages 22-3)
400 g (14 oz) sugar
2 teaspoons cold water
cornflour for sprinkling
30 cm (12 inch) fluted round silver cake card
pink food colouring pen
225 g (8 oz) sugared almonds

The Sugar Plum Fairy Castle assembled and completed

Preparation time: 1 hour, plus cooling, drying
Cooking time: 40 minutes
Oven: 180°C, 350°F, Gas Mark 4

1. Place two-thirds of the whisked sponge mixture in a greased, greaseproof paper-lined 33 × 23 cm (13 × 9 inch) Swiss Roll tin, and one third of the mixture in a greased, greaseproof paper-lined 28 × 18 cm (11 × 7 inch) Swiss Roll tin. Bake in a preheated oven for 15-20 minutes until well risen and firm to the touch.
2. Use some of the apricot glaze as filling and roll up following the instructions for making a Swiss roll (page 24) but roll the smaller Swiss Roll

lengthways to make a long thin roll.

3. Make the fondant moulding paste and tint it very pale pink with a few drops of food colouring, then wrap it in cling film.

4. Place the quick mix cake mixture in a greased, greaseproof paper-lined 20 cm (8 inch) sandwich tin and bake in a preheated oven for 15-20 minutes until well risen and firm to touch. Turn out and cool on a wire tray.

5. Place the sugar in a bowl, add a drop of pink food colouring to tint it the same colour as the fondant moulding paste. Reserve one third of the sugar and add the water to the remainder. Mix well together so that the sugar becomes damp.

6. Make 3 cone shapes out of paper (see small picture, right). Fill the large cone with the dampened sugar and press firmly down. Place a piece of card over the top and invert the sugar cone, then remove the paper shape. Repeat to make 1 medium and 2 small cones and leave in a warm place to dry hard.

7. Trim the ends of each Swiss Roll, so that they are level. Cut one third off each roll to make 4 towers all of different heights (see diagram, right).

8. Unwrap the moulding paste and cut into 5 pieces. Roll out one piece thinly on a surface well sprinkled with cornflour, the width of the largest roll and long enough to roll completely around it.

9. Brush the roll with some of the remaining apricot glaze, place it on the moulding paste, trim the moulding paste to fit, then roll up, carefully sealing the join well by rubbing over it with cornfloured fingers. Repeat to cover the remaining rolls. Knead and re-roll the trimmings.

10. Place the reserved sugar on a piece of greaseproof paper and roll each iced roll in it to coat evenly. Leave to dry.

11. Place the round cake on the cake board and, using plain cutters the same size as the base of each roll, cut out and remove 4 rounds.

12. Brush the cake with some more of the apricot glaze and roll out the remaining moulding paste to a circle

large enough to cover the round cake. Place the moulding paste over the cake, and gently press it into the holes. Smooth over and trim off the excess at the base. Sprinkle the moulding paste and cake board with the remaining pink-tinted sugar.

13. Place each pink tower in position in the cut-out holes and carefully place the sugar cones on top of each.

14. Make the windows and doors for the towers with the fondant moulding paste trimmings (as in the main picture) and use the pink pen to mark the lattice work and door panels. Place these in position and secure with the remaining apricot glaze.

15. Arrange the sugared almonds like a path and steps into the castle.

Using a paper cone to make the castle's sugar towers

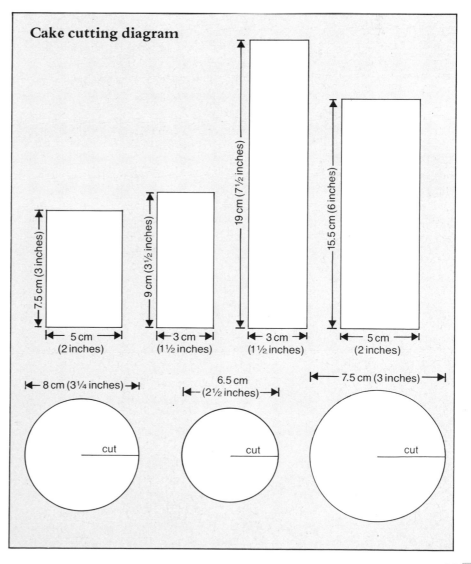

Cake cutting diagram

7.5 cm (3 inches) · 5 cm (2 inches)

9 cm (3½ inches) · 3 cm (1½ inches)

19 cm (7½ inches) · 3 cm (1½ inches)

15.5 cm (6 inches) · 5 cm (2 inches)

8 cm (3¼ inches)

6.5 cm (2½ inches)

7.5 cm (3 inches)

cut · cut · cut

WINDOW BOX

3-egg quantity Quick Mix Cake
    mixture (pages 22-3)
½ quantity Fondant Moulding Paste
    (page 36)
green, pink, yellow and orange food
    colourings
cornflour
½ quantity Chocolate Butter Cream
    (page 38)
20 cm (8 inch) square silver cake board
2 × 150 g (5 oz) packets chocolate
    finger biscuits

Preparation time: 1 hour, plus
                            drying
Cooking time: 50-55 minutes
Oven: 170°C, 325°F, Gas
                     Mark 3

Orange flowers with green
centres made from fondant
moulding paste

The fondant moulding paste
pieces needed to make the pink
and yellow flowers

1. Place the cake mixture in a greased
and lined 1 kg (2 lb) loaf tin and bake in
a preheated oven for 50-55 minutes
until well risen and firm to the touch.
Turn out, remove paper and cool on a
wire tray.
2. Make the fondant moulding paste.
Divide the moulding paste into 4 equal
portions and colour each piece with a
few drops of food colouring, so that
the portions are tinted green, pink,
yellow and orange.
3. Roll out the green moulding paste.
Cut out 20 leaves, marking the veins
with a knife, bend slightly, then leave
to dry on a plate dusted with cornflour.
Re-roll the trimmings.
4. To make 22 pink flowers (see
picture, bottom left), take small balls of
the pink moulding paste, then press out
3 round petal shapes for each flower
between thumb and forefinger. Fold
the petals inwards, then gently press
the 3 petals together to complete the
flower and leave to set.
5. Using the yellow moulding paste,
press out 20 larger yellow petals and
fold inwards, leaving a stem attached
(see picture, bottom left). Next take the
orange moulding paste and press out
into 12 large round shapes with a stem
and press a green piece, taken from the
leaf trimmings, into each centre (see

picture, top left). Leave all the flowers
and leaves to set hard.
6. Make the chocolate butter cream
and spread evenly over the sides and
top of the cake. Place on the cake
board.

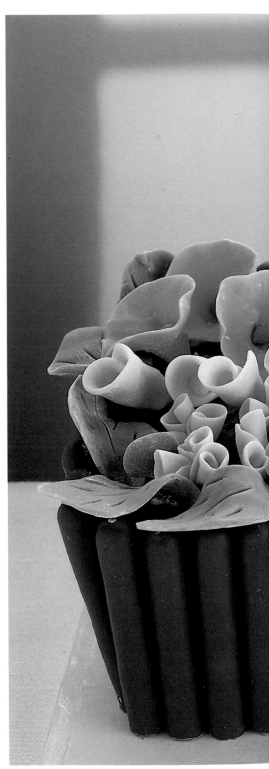

7. Trim and fit the chocolate finger biscuits all around the sides of the cake, leaving the fingers at the back the full length as these will be needed to support the large orange flowers at the back of the box.

8. Arrange the leaves around the front and side edges of the window box. Place the pink flowers at the front, then arrange the yellow flowers next, with the large orange flowers at the back, supported by the chocolate fingers.

The Window Box full of a fine array of flowers and leaves

EXECUTIVE CASE

3-egg quantity Coffee Quick Mix Cake
  mixture (pages 22-3)
1 quantity Fondant Moulding Paste
  (page 36)
violet, blue, red and gold food
  colourings
2 tablespoons Apricot Glaze (page 30)
20 cm (8 inch) square thin silver cake
  board
1 oblong wafer biscuit
black edible food colouring pen
1 blackcurrant candy stick
2 sheets of rice paper

Preparation time: 10 minutes, plus
                    setting
Cooking time: 50-55 minutes
Oven: 170°C, 325°F, Gas
                    Mark 3

1. Place the cake mixture in a greased
and lined 26 × 19 cm (10½ × 7½ inch)
oblong tin, 5 cm (2 inches) deep and
bake in a preheated oven for 50-55
minutes until well risen and firm to the
touch. Turn out of the tin, remove the
paper and cool on a wire tray.
2. Make the moulding paste. Reserve a
small piece and colour the remainder a

The Executive Case and its
accessories

brown-burgundy colour by adding violet, blue and red food colourings.

3. Cut the cake in half across the width, sandwich together with apricot glaze and trim the top square. Brush with apricot glaze and place on the cake board.

4. Roll out one third of the burgundy coloured moulding paste to a 13 cm (5 inch) square. Cut the square in half and place each piece down the side of the case. Trim to fit.

5. Roll out the remaining piece of burgundy paste large enough to cover the case. Carefully fit the paste over the case and trim to fit, neatly joining the edges together.

6. Mark a line across the top and down the side for the opening seam.

7. Cover the biscuit with trimmings of burgundy moulding paste for the handle and roll, cut and trim a 4 cm (1½ inch) square for the label.

8. Roll out the white moulding paste and cut out 2 locks, 2 handle supports and the initials and paint with gold food colouring. Leave to set. Cut out the name tag from white paste. Reserve the trimmings. (See diagram, below right.)

9. Secure the locks in place with a little glaze, and the handle and supports. Write, with a food colouring pen, the name and address of the person, then stick together with the label.

10. Fix the label in position under the handle.

11. Re-roll the burgundy moulding paste trimmings into a 15 cm (6 inch) round. Place the candy stick in the centre, then pleat the remaining paste around like an umbrella (see pictures, right).

12. With the remaining white icing, make a handle and top for the umbrella and trim with gold paint. Leave to set, then place on the cake board.

13. Using the rice paper and colouring pen, make a newspaper and write the day and date of the celebration, favourite newspaper title and a few lines written in columns. Place by the case.

The pieces of burgundy-coloured fondant moulding paste and the candy stick used to make the umbrella

Pleating up the circle of fondant moulding paste for the umbrella

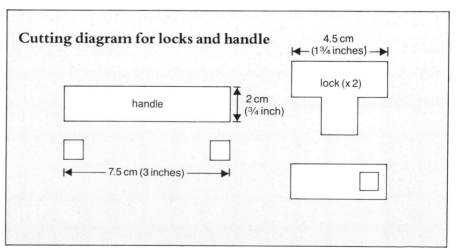

Cutting diagram for locks and handle

handle

7.5 cm (3 inches)

2 cm (¾ inch)

4.5 cm (1¾ inches)

lock (x 2)

TREASURE ISLAND

3-egg quantity Quick Mix Cake
  mixture (pages 22-3)
1 quantity Fudge Frosting (page 39)
25 cm (10 inch) thin round silver cake
  board
2 tablespoons demerara sugar
blue and green decorating gels
2 jelly feet
1 jelly crocodile
5 curl biscuits
1 tablespoon coconut
50 g (2 oz) Marzipan (page 30)
green food colouring
5 pieces Swiss milk chocolate with soft
  filling
milk chocolate coins
jelly sweets
gold and silver almonds
2.5 cm (1 inch) square rice paper
black food colouring pen

Preparation time: 40 minutes
Cooking time: 40-45 minutes
Oven: 170°C, 325°F, Gas
Mark 3

1. Place the cake mixture in a greased and lined 28 × 18 cm (11 × 7 inch) oblong tin, 4 cm (1½ inches) deep and bake in a preheated oven for 40-45 minutes until well risen and firm to the touch. Turn out, remove the paper and cool on a wire tray.
2. Cut pieces out of the cake to give it an island shape and place on to the cake board. Reserve the pieces.
3. Make the fudge frosting. Spread about two-thirds of the frosting evenly all over the top and sides of the cake.
4. Spread the remaining cake pieces with frosting and arrange around and on top of the cake to resemble rocks.
5. Sprinkle the demerara sugar around the cake board and on the rocks at the base of the cake. Squeeze the blue gel on the remaining cake board to make the sea.
6. Squeeze some green gel over the rocks by the sea edge for seaweed. Place the jelly feet as footprints in the sand and the crocodile in the sea.
7. Press the curl biscuits into the top of

the cake by the rocks to make tree trunks. Colour the coconut green with a few drops of food colouring, and then spoon the coconut round the trees.
8. Colour the marzipan green with food colouring and mould 15-18 palm leaves and snip the sides with a pair of scissors. Gently push 2 or 3 leaves into the top of each tree trunk to attach.
9. Using a little frosting, stick 4 pieces of chocolate together to make a chest and press into the centre of the cake. Place the remaining piece of chocolate resting at the side for a lid.
10. Fill the chest with the chocolate coins, jelly sweets and almonds and press some extras into the cake.
11. Make a map out of rice paper, using the edible food colouring pen.

Left: the Treasure Island cake; right: Beach Time and the umbrellas are up on the sands

BEACH TIME

3-egg quantity Quick Mix Cake
   mixture (pages 22-3)
1 quantity Butter Cream (page 38)
blue food colouring
30 cm (12 inch) square cake board
225 g (8 oz) assorted nuts coated in
   white milk chocolate, or raisins
   coated in yogurt
2 tablespoons demerara sugar
20 orange sticks
3 cocktail umbrellas
1 strip strawberry-flavoured liquorice
2 large and 3 small jelly babies
2 pairs of jelly trainers
2 jelly mermaids

Preparation time: 40 minutes
Cooking time: 40-45 minutes
Oven: 170°C, 325°F, Gas
                       Mark 3

1. Place the cake mixture in a greased
and lined 28 × 18 cm (11 × 7 inch)
oblong tin, 4 cm (1½ inches) deep and
bake in a preheated oven for 40-45
minutes until well risen and firm to the
touch. Turn out, remove the paper and
cool on a wire tray.
2. Make the butter cream and colour
one third pale blue.
3. Cut the cake according to the
diagram left. Place the deep part of the
cake at the back of the cake board and
invert the second piece at the front.
4. Spread two-thirds of the cake with
plain butter cream evenly over the
sides, back and top. Press the nuts or
raisins into the top third of the cake to
represent the pebbled part of the beach.
5. Sprinkle the centre with demerara
sugar as sand, and spread the blue
butter cream on the remaining cake in
peaks as the sea.
6. For breakwaters, press 12 orange
sticks, spaced apart, down 2 opposite
sides of the cake and using a little plain
butter cream secure the remaining
sticks in between.
7. Place the cocktail umbrellas,
liquorice beach mats, jelly babies,
trainers and mermaids to create a lively
beach scene.

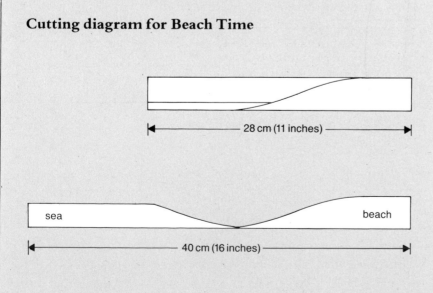

Cutting diagram for Beach Time

28 cm (11 inches)

sea — beach

40 cm (16 inches)

Using a template as a guide to cutting out the dough frames for the aquarium sides

Colouring the dough frames before baking them

Opposite: the completed Tropical Aquarium

TROPICAL AQUARIUM

2-egg quantity Quick Mix Cake mixture (pages 22-3)
1 quantity Biscuit Dough, reserving the remaining egg white (see Christmas Tree Cookies, page 134)
250 g (8 oz) glacier mint sweets
blue, orange and green food colourings
½ quantity Chocolate Butter Cream (page 38)
20 cm (8 inch) thin silver cake board
50 g (2 oz) Marzipan (page 30)
2 tablespoons rainbow mix or hundreds and thousands

Preparation time: 50 minutes, plus cooling
Cooking time: 40-45 minutes
Oven: 180°C, 350°F, Gas Mark 4

1. Place the cake mixture in a greased and lined 28 × 18 cm (11 × 7 inch) Swiss roll tin and bake in a preheated oven for 30-35 minutes until well risen and firm to the touch. Turn out, remove the paper and cool on a wire tray.
2. Make the biscuit dough and roll out on a baking sheet lined with non-stick silicone paper.
3. Using templates (see diagram below), cut out dough frames. Knead the centre pieces and trimmings together and use to make the last frames.

Place 15 sweets, spaced evenly apart, in the centre of each large biscuit dough frame and 10 sweets in the small frames.
4. Mix the egg white with a little blue food colouring and glaze the dough frames evenly. Bake in the oven for 8-10 minutes until the sweets have melted and filled the frames. Cool on the paper, then remove carefully and leave on a wire tray until cold.
5. Make the butter cream. Cut a piece of cake 20 × 15 cm (8 × 6 inches) and spread evenly with most of the butter cream icing.
6. Place the cake in the centre of a cake board. Press the 2 smaller biscuit pieces on to the short sides of the cake. Secure with extra icing if necessary.
7. Place the large biscuit pieces in position on the long sides, spreading with a little extra icing before fitting.
8. Knead some orange food colouring into half of the marzipan and green colouring into the remainder, making light and dark green pieces of marzipan. Shape the orange marzipan into fish shapes and the green into shaded rock plants.
9. Cut up the remaining cake into pieces and spread with the remaining icing. Arrange like rocks in the aquarium. Sprinkle the rainbow mixture or hundreds and thousands over the bottom and arrange the fish and rock plants.

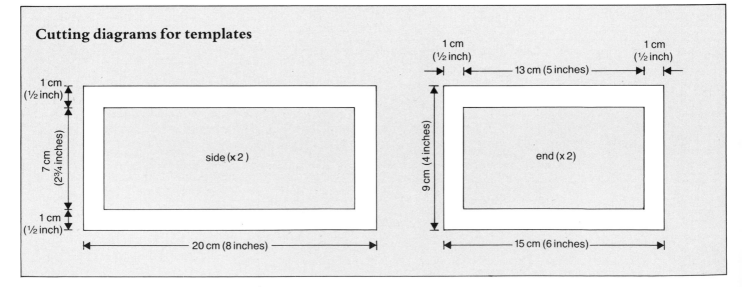

Cutting diagrams for templates

1 cm (½ inch)

7 cm (2¾ inches)

1 cm (½ inch)

side (×2)

20 cm (8 inches)

1 cm (½ inch)   13 cm (5 inches)   1 cm (½ inch)

9 cm (4 inches)

end (×2)

15 cm (6 inches)

GOLF COURSE

3-egg quantity Quick Mix Cake
  mixture (pages 22-3)
1 quantity Butter Cream (page 38)
green, brown and black food
  colourings
50 g (2 oz) desiccated coconut
30 cm (12 inch) thin square silver cake
  board
2 tablespoons light soft brown sugar
20 orange sticks
small piece of red paper
1 sweet cigarette
1 tablespoon plain chocolate dots,
  melted
5 curl biscuits
75 g (3 oz) Marzipan (page 30)

Preparation time: 50 minutes, plus
                      setting
Cooking time: 40-45 minutes
Oven: 170°C, 325°F, Gas
                      Mark 3

1. Place the cake mixture in a greased
and lined 28 × 18 cm (11 × 7 inch)
cake tin, 4 cm (1½ inches) deep. Bake
in a preheated oven for 40-45 minutes
until well risen and firm to the touch.
Turn out, remove the paper and cool
on a wire tray.
2. Make the butter cream and colour it
green. Place the coconut in a polythene
bag with a few drops of green food
colouring and shake well to colour
evenly.
3. Cut a sloping piece of cake out of
the front corner as a bunker. Spread the
butter cream icing over the cake to
cover it completely, spreading the
centre evenly. Cut the spare piece of
cake into 3, cover each with icing and
arrange around the top of the cake as
landscaping.
4. Place a 10 cm (4 inch) plain cutter in
the centre, then carefully sprinkle the
coconut all over the top and sides of the
cake, keeping the centre clear. This
makes the green.
5. Place the cake on the cake board and
sprinkle the sugar over the bunker to
cover it evenly. Carefully remove the
cutter.

6. Press the orange sticks in position
around the outside of the cake for
fencing. Cut out a flag shape from the
red paper, attach it to the sweet
cigarette and position it in the green.
Make a hole near the flag with a straw
or something slim.
7. Spread the melted chocolate over
the curl biscuits to coat evenly, leave
until set, then press into the cake at the
back at different angles for tree trunks.
8. Colour the marzipan green with a
few drops of green food colouring.
Press out irregular round shapes, fold
and press into the tree trunks, to
represent the leaves.
9. Roll a tiny ball of plain marzipan
and place on the green, then divide the
remaining marzipan and colour grey
and brown with food colouring. Press
into different shaped golf clubs (brown
marzipan) and a carrying bag (grey
marzipan).
10. Leave to set until firm, then place
by the green.

Left, Golf Course cake; right:
Table Tennis Bat

TABLE TENNIS BAT

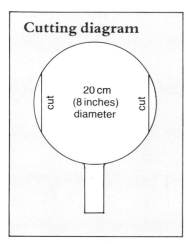

Cutting diagram

20 cm
(8 inches)
diameter

cut

cut

2-egg Chocolate Quick Mix Cake
  mixture (page 23)
225 g (8 oz) Fondant Moulding Paste
  (page 36)
brown and red food colourings
100 g (4 oz) Marzipan (page 30)
2 tablespoons Apricot Glaze (page 30)
1 mini chocolate roll
icing sugar for sprinkling
30 cm (12 inch) round silver cake
  board

Preparation time: 30 minutes
Cooking time: 40–45 minutes
Oven: 170°C, 325°F, Gas
    Mark 3

1. Place the cake mixture in a greased
and base-lined 20 cm (8 inch) sandwich
tin and bake in a preheated oven for 40–
45 minutes or until well risen and firm
to the touch. Turn out and cool on a
wire tray.

2. Make the moulding paste, cut off a
piece and make a table tennis ball.
Colour the remainder light brown by
kneading in a few drops of brown food
colouring. Colour the marzipan red
with a few drops of red colouring.
3. Trim the edges off each side of the
cake, as in the diagram left. Brush with
some of the apricot glaze and place on
the cake board.
4. Place the mini roll in position for the
handle, putting the cake trimmings
underneath to make it level with the
cake. Use some apricot glaze to stick
them together.
5. Roll out some of the brown
moulding paste on a work surface well
sprinkled with icing sugar, making it
large enough to cover the bat. Re-roll
the trimmings. Carefully lift into
position and smooth the icing all over.
6. Trim off the excess icing and neaten
the edges. Roll out the marzipan and
trim to an 18 cm (7 inch) round. Mark
a pattern on to the surface like a table
tennis bat by pressing the coarse side of
a grater on to the marzipan.
7. Place the marzipan in position on
the bat and mould to the edge. Knead
the trimmings together, roll out and
cut into a thin strip to place around the
base of the cake.
8. Roll the remaining brown icing into
a shape to fit the handle and press
gently in position. Place the ball on the
bat.

DENNIS DINOSAUR

2-egg quantity Quick Mix Cake
    mixture (pages 22-3)
peppermint essence
green food colouring
1 quantity Fondant Moulding Paste
    (page 36)
2 tablespoons Apricot Glaze (page 30)
2 mini chocolate Swiss rolls
3 sweet cigarettes
red dragees
2 strips strawberry flavour liquorice

Preparation time: 45 minutes, plus
    setting
Cooking time: 40-45 minutes
Oven: 170°C, 325°F, Gas
    Mark 3

1. Make the cake mixture according to
the instructions (pages 22-3), adding a
few drops of peppermint essence and
green food colouring.
2. Place the mixture in a greased and
base-lined 20 cm (8 inch) round
sandwich tin and bake in a preheated
oven for 40-45 minutes until well risen
and firm to the touch. Turn out,
remove the paper and cool on a wire
tray.
3. Make the fondant moulding paste
and colour it green with a few drops of
food colouring.
4. Using a 7.5 cm (3 inch) plain cutter,
cut a round out from the centre of the
cake and remove. Cut the cake into 2
half circles and sandwich together with
some of the apricot glaze, following the
diagram opposite.

Attaching the dinosaur's head
to the body, using cigarette
sweets as a base

5. Roll out two-thirds of the fondant
moulding paste and cover the cake
completely, carefully sealing the joins
underneath the arched body shape.
6. Cut the mini Swiss rolls in half to
make 4 legs and cut the remaining
round piece of cake in half. Use one
half for a head then cut the other semi-
circle in half for the tail pieces, as in the
diagram below.
7. Roll out the remaining moulding
paste and carefully cover the legs, head
and tail pieces. Leave all the pieces to
set for at least 1 hour in a warm place or

preferably overnight.
8. Arrange the legs on a long board or
tray and brush the tops with some of
the remaining apricot glaze. Place the
body in position.
9. Press 2 sweet cigarettes a little way
into the head end and one into the tail
end, brush the head and one tail piece
with glaze at one end and press into
position on the body. Attach the
remaining tail piece with glaze.
10. Using red dragees, press into the
head for eyes and mouth. Cut the
liquorice strips in half, then into

Left: Dennis Dinosaur

diamond shapes. Press these into the icing all over the head, back and tail to represent spines.

11. Cut the remaining pieces of liquorice into tiny toe nails and stick them around the feet with the remaining apricot glaze.

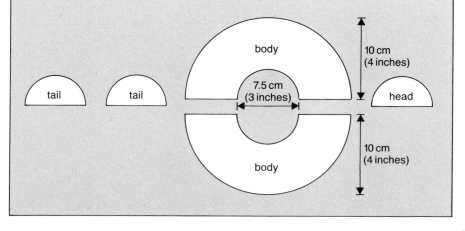

tail

tail

body

7.5 cm
(3 inches)

body

10 cm
(4 inches)

10 cm
(4 inches)

head

SAMMY SNAKE

3-egg quantity Whisked Sponge Cake mixture (pages 24-5)
3 tablespoons Apricot Glaze (page 30)
1 quantity Fondant Moulding Paste (page 36)
blue, green and orange food colourings
2 orange jelly diamonds
2 green jelly diamonds, cut in half

Preparation time: 25 minutes, plus cooling
Cooking time: 10-15 minutes
Oven: 180°C, 350°F, Gas Mark 4

Rolling up the long edges of the Swiss roll, using a rolling pin as a support

The rolled-up cake ready for bending into Sammy Snake's shape

1. Place the cake mixture in a greased and lined 33 × 23 cm (13 × 9 inch) Swiss roll tin and bake in a preheated oven for 10-15 minutes until well risen and firm to the touch.
2. Turn the cake out on to a piece of sugared greaseproof paper. Remove lining paper and trim off the edges.
3. Quickly brush with some of the apricot glaze and roll up one long edge to the centre. Place a rolling pin behind as a support. Roll the opposite edge into the centre.
4. Leave to set for a couple of minutes, then cut the cake in half down the centre to make 2 long thin rolls. Place the rolls on a cooling rack and bend each roll into an 'S' shape.
5. Make the fondant moulding paste and colour three-quarters of it turquoise blue using a few drops of blue and green food colourings.
6. Colour the remaining moulding paste orange. Place the 2 rolls on a long tray or board and brush the 2 ends with glaze to join them together.
7. Brush the roll all over with glaze, then roll out the turquoise blue moulding paste into a long thin strip 2.5 cm (1 inch) longer than the snake. Cover the snake with the moulding paste, shaping it carefully to form the tail at one end and the head at the other and pressing gently to fit.
8. Slit the icing at the head end to form the mouth. Use a little of the orange icing to line the mouth and to make a forked tongue; place it in the mouth.
9. Roll the remaining orange moulding paste and cut into thin strips. Cut the strips into short lengths and arrange at intervals across the body as stripes. Cut 2 dots for the eyes and place in position.
10. Use the green jelly diamonds for teeth. Place the orange jelly diamonds on the head.

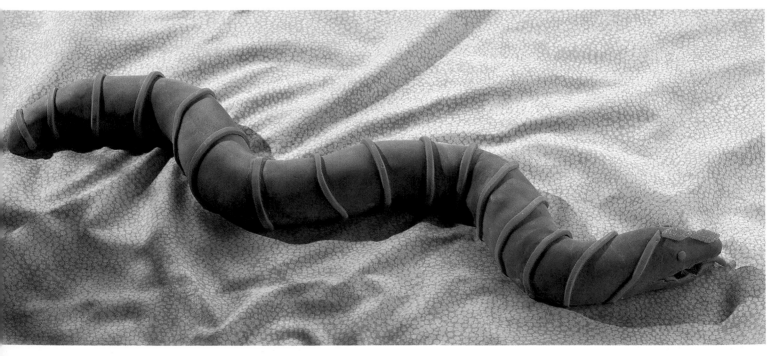

1. Place the cake mixture in a greased and lined 28 × 18 cm (11 × 7 inch) oblong tin, 4 cm (1½ inches) deep and bake in a preheated oven for 50-55 minutes until well risen and firm to the touch. Turn out, remove the paper and cool on a wire tray.
2. Cut out the cake according to the diagram below and assemble the pieces in the correct order.
3. Make the fondant moulding paste and colour one third red and two-thirds grey with a few drops of red and black food colourings.
4. Roll out the red paste thinly, brush the booster jets and body with apricot glaze, then cover each piece with red moulding paste and trim to fit. Using some grey moulding paste, roll and cut out the trims for the body and place in position.
5. Roll out the remaining grey icing and cover all the remaining parts of the transformer, glazing them first with apricot glaze. Trim the head and arms with a strip of red icing.
6. Arrange the pieces in order on the cake board.

TOBY TRANSFORMER

3-egg quantity Quick Mix Cake
   mixture (pages 22-3)
1 quantity Fondant Moulding Paste
   (page 36)
red and black food colourings
2 tablespoons Apricot Glaze (page 30)
30 cm (12 inch) thin square silver cake
   board

Preparation time:	45 minutes, plus setting
Cooking time:	50-55 minutes
Oven:	170°C, 325°F, Gas Mark 3

Opposite: Sammy Snake; above: Toby Transformer

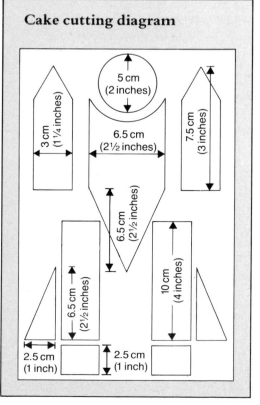

Cake cutting diagram

5 cm (2 inches)

3 cm (1¼ inches)

6.5 cm (2½ inches)

7.5 cm (3 inches)

6.5 cm (2½ inches)

6.5 cm (2½ inches)

10 cm (4 inches)

2.5 cm (1 inch)

2.5 cm (1 inch)

OVER THE RAINBOW

2-egg quantity Quick Mix Cake
  mixture (pages 22-3)
1 quantity Fondant Moulding Paste
  (page 36)
red, yellow, blue, green and violet food
  colourings
2 tablespoons Apricot Glaze (page 30)
cornflour for dusting
25 g (1 oz) desiccated coconut

30 cm (12 inch) thin silver cake board
flowers made from Fondant Moulding
  Paste to decorate (optional)

Preparation time: 30 minutes
Cooking time: 35-40 minutes
Oven: 170°C, 325°F, Gas
Mark 3

The three cakes made from the
Over the Rainbow recipe

1. Place the cake mixture in a greased
and base-lined 20 cm (8 inch) sandwich

tin in a preheated oven for 35–40 minutes until well risen and firm to the touch. Turn out, remove the paper and cool on a wire tray.

2. Make the fondant moulding paste and divide it into 8 pieces. Using the food colourings to blend the colours, colour one piece red, one orange (with yellow and red), one yellow, one blue, one indigo (with blue and a little violet) and one piece violet, leaving one piece white. Wrap each piece separately in cling film until required.

3. Using a 7.5 cm (3 inch) plain cutter, cut a round out of the centre of the cake and remove. Cut the cake and the small round in half. (See small pictures, right.) Reserve the 2 small semi-circles of cake.

4. Sandwich the rainbow shapes together with apricot glaze. Brush the underside of the rainbow with glaze.

5. Roll out the white moulding paste and cover the arch underneath the rainbow. Trim to fit. Place the rainbow the right way up and brush with glaze.

6. Dust the work surface with plenty of cornflour and roll out the red moulding paste, then cut a strip, about 1 cm (½ inch) wide. Place over the centre join of the cake and trim to fit. Knead the trimmings together.

7. Repeat to roll out the orange moulding paste and cut out 2 strips and place one on either side of the red strip. Trim to fit, kneading the trimmings.

8. Continue to cut out 2 yellow, 2 green, 2 blue, 2 indigo and 2 violet strips. Carefully apply them to each side of the cake. Trim to fit and knead all the trimmings together, keeping the colours separate.

9. Repeat, if wished, to cover the remaining semi-circles to make 2 mini rainbows.

10. If liked, serve the rainbow cakes set out on a cake board. Brush the cake board with apricot glaze. Colour the coconut green with a few drops of food colouring and sprinkle all over the board to cover evenly.

11. Any trimmings of the coloured fondant moulding paste may also be used, if liked, to make moulded flowers to decorate the desiccated coconut 'grass' on the cake board. Press out small petal shapes from the trimmings, join 3 petals together and trim off the stalks.

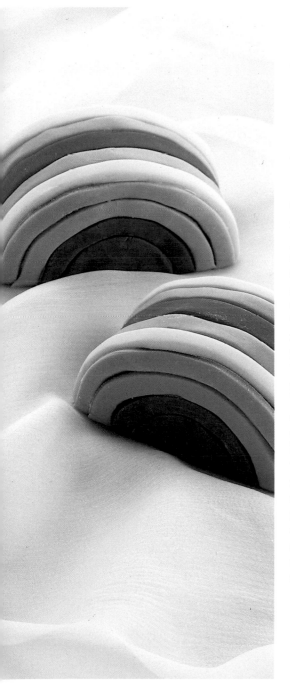

The cake cut into rainbow shapes; a 7.5 mm (3 inch) cutter was used for the centre cut

Fitting the central red strip of fondant moulding paste over the cake

BALLET SHOES

3-egg quantity Whisked Sponge Cake
   mixture (pages 24-5)
3 tablespoons Apricot Glaze (page 30)
1 quantity Fondant Moulding Paste
   (page 36)
pink and yellow food colourings
4 ice cream wafers
1 metre (1 yard) peach ribbon, 1 cm
   (½ inch) wide
20 cm (8 inch) round thin silver cake
   board

Preparation time: 30 minutes
Cooking time: 10-15 minutes
Oven: 180°C, 350°F, Gas
                  Mark 4

How to use the fondant moulding paste

As the Swiss roll is very fragile when it is first made, leave it to settle for a day before making the ballet shoes.

When rolling out the fondant moulding paste, take care not to roll it out too thinly, otherwise the cake may show through and the moulding paste will be difficult to handle when it is being moulded into the shape of the ballet shoes.

1. Place the cake mixture in a greased and lined 33 × 23 cm (13 × 9 inch) Swiss roll tin and bake in a preheated oven for 10-15 minutes until well risen and firm to the touch.
2. Turn the cake out on to a piece of sugared greaseproof paper. Remove the lining paper and trim off the edges of the cake.
3. Quickly spread with some of the apricot glaze and roll up from the long edge. Cool on a wire tray.
4. Make the moulding icing and add a few drops of pink and yellow food colourings to make it peach-coloured.
5. Cut the wafers out to form the soles of the shoes. Cut the Swiss roll in half and press one end of each into a point.
6. Cut out a shallow oval shape from the centre of each roll, then brush both all over with most of the remaining glaze.
7. Cut the icing in half and roll out one half large enough to cover one roll. Use this icing to cover one of the rolls completely, join on the undersides, and neaten the edges. Shape the heel and toe of the shoe until smooth.
8. Brush the wafer sole with glaze and press into position on the ballet shoe, trimming to fit if necessary. Using well-cornfloured hands, press the icing into the oval depression in the centre of the shoe and form a sharp edge all around the top with the fingers.

9. Make an icing bow from the peach icing trimmings. Make into a pencil-thin roll, fold into two loops, trim and place in position on the toe with glaze. Repeat steps 7 to 9 for the other shoe.
10. Cut the ribbon into 4 pieces; press in position at the back of each shoe and secure with icing. Arrange the ballet

shoes on the cake board.
11. Petal candle holders, made from icing trimmings, may be made for this cake, if liked. Take a small ball of icing and press into a petal shape, curl the edge of the petal inwards to form a centre. Press out another petal shape and wrap around the centre petal; repeat with a third petal, then cut off the stem. Press the candle into the centre. Repeat to make as many candle holders as required, then place beside the ballet shoes.

Matching ribbon ties complete the Ballet Shoes cake

FESTIVE LANTERN

1 egg white, beaten
red, green and yellow food colourings
1½ quantities Biscuit Dough (see
    Christmas Tree Cookies, page 134)
12 yellow and 12 orange thin boiled
    fruit sweets
18 cm (7 inch) square cake board
4 tablespoons Royal Icing (page 32)
50 g (2 oz) liquorice comfits
½ metre (½ yard) each red and green
    ribbons, 2.5 cm (1 inch) wide

Preparation time: 45-50 minutes,
plus setting
Cooking time: 10-15 minutes
Oven: 170°C, 325°F, Gas
Mark 3

1. Make the templates for the lantern following the diagram below. Divide the egg white into 3 and colour one portion red, one green and one yellow.
2. Make the biscuit dough.
3. Roll out one quarter of the dough thinly on a baking sheet lined with non-stick silicone paper. Using the templates, cut one base and a side piece to make a frame, then place 4 sweets a little apart in the centre of the frame.
4. Brush the base and frames with alternate stripes of coloured glaze. Bake in a preheated oven for 10-15 minutes until the sweets have melted and filled the centre. Cool on the paper, then remove carefully and place on a wire tray.
5. Repeat to make 3 more side pieces with 4 sweets each, 4 triangular pieces with 2 sweets each and an open ring for the top. When the pieces are cold, wrap them in cling film until required.
6. Place the lantern base on the cake board, put the icing into a greaseproof paper piping bag, snip off the end and pipe the edges with icing. Pipe some icing down the long sides of each side piece, then stick on to the base to form a box, gently pressing the side together. Leave to set for several hours.
7. Assemble the top of the lantern by piping some icing on 2 sides of each triangle, but not the base. Using an egg cup as a support, fit the 4 triangles together, press gently to hold, then leave to set for several hours or overnight.
8. Pipe a line of icing around the top of the lantern body. Attach the top of the lantern to the body and secure the ring on top with a little icing. Leave to set.
9. Use icing to secure the liquorice comfits down the joins on the top.
10. Thread the ribbons through the ring, if liked.

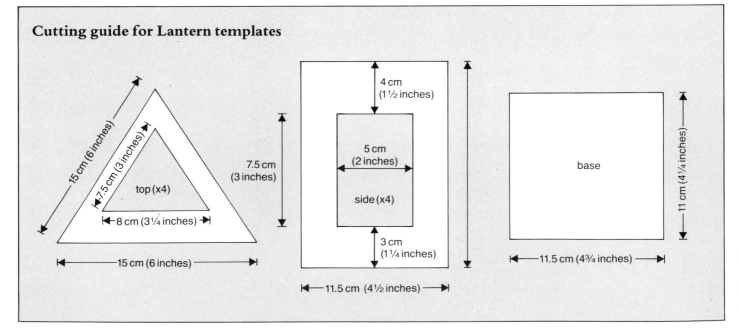

Cutting guide for Lantern templates

15 cm (6 inches)
7.5 cm (3 inches)
top (x4)
8 cm (3¼ inches)
15 cm (6 inches)

4 cm (1½ inches)
5 cm (2 inches)
side (x4)
7.5 cm (3 inches)
3 cm (1¼ inches)
11.5 cm (4½ inches)

base
11 cm (4¼ inches)
11.5 cm (4¾ inches)

The windows of the Festive
Lantern are lit by the bright
colours of the melted sweets
from which the 'glass' is made

HAPPILY RETIRED

3-egg quantity Lemon Quick Mix
 Cake mixture (pages 22-3)
1 quantity Fondant Moulding Paste
 (page 36)
yellow and brown food colourings
2 tablespoons Apricot Glaze (page 30)
25 cm (10 inch) thin round silver cake
 board
black edible food colouring pen

Preparation time: 45 minutes
Cooking time: 50-55 minutes
Oven: 170°C, 325°F, Gas
           Mark 3

1. Place the cake mixture in a greased
and lined 26 × 16 cm (10½ × 7½ inch)
oblong cake tin, 5 cm (2 inches) deep.
Bake in a preheated oven for 50-55
minutes until well risen and firm to the
touch. Turn out, remove the paper and
cool on a wire tray.
2. Make the fondant moulding paste,
then colour two thirds of it streaky
yellow by kneading until coloured in
streaks (see small pictures, opposite),
and one third brown with a few drops
of the food colourings.
3. Cut the cake and assemble like a
chair, according to the diagram below.
Use the cake trimmings to cut out a
small cushion and a book.
4. Brush the back and seat pieces with

Opposite: the Happily Retired
cake assembled on a cake
board

apricot glaze and press together. Place
on the cake board. Roll out about one
third of the yellow moulding paste,
large enough to cover the seat, front
and back of the chair. Place the
moulding paste over the cake, press in
position and trim to fit. Press the
trimmings together.
5. Roll out another third of the
moulding paste and cut out 4 side arm

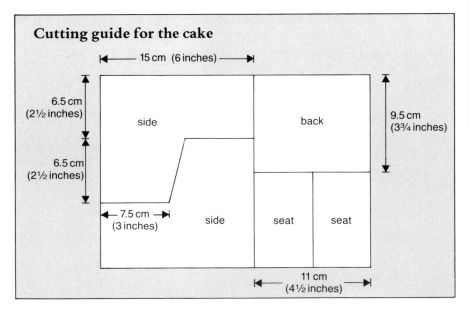

Cutting guide for the cake

15 cm (6 inches)

6.5 cm (2½ inches)

side

back

9.5 cm (3¾ inches)

6.5 cm (2½ inches)

7.5 cm (3 inches)

side

seat

seat

11 cm (4½ inches)

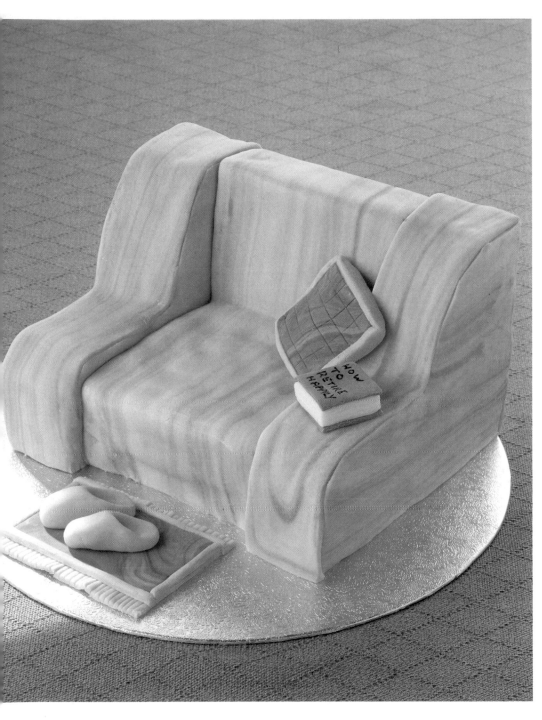

Starting to roll the yellow
colouring into the fondant
moulding paste

Folding and rolling the
fondant moulding paste to
achieve a streaky colour effect

pieces using the cake shape as a
template. Brush the outside of the arm
pieces with glaze and press the
moulding paste on to each side, then
brush the top of the arm pieces with
apricot glaze.

6. Press the arm pieces in position.
Roll out 2 long strips of yellow
moulding paste to cover the top of
each, press in position and trim.

7. Roll out the brown moulding paste
and use to cover the cushion and book
case pieces. Use a little more to make a
rug and trim it with yellow. Mould the
slippers out of scraps of yellow fondant
moulding paste.

8. Using an edible food colouring pen,
write the book title on the cover: 'How
to Retire Happily', or similar, and
assemble the chair and its accessories.

115

BUNNY BIG EARS

2-egg quantity Quick Mix Cake
   mixture (pages 22–3)
50 g (2 oz) chocolate dots
175 g (6 oz) Fondant Moulding Paste
   (page 36)
orange, blue and green food colourings
1 quantity Butter Cream (page 38)
25 g (1 oz) desiccated coconut
2 tablespoons Apricot Glaze (page 30)
20 cm (8 inch) round thin silver cake
   board
1 sheet of rice paper
1 blue food colouring pen

Preparation time: 30 minutes, plus
                     setting
Cooking time: 40–45 minutes
Oven: 170°C, 325°F, Gas
                  Mark 3

1. Make the quick mix cake mixture
and stir in the chocolate dots. Place in a
greased and base-lined 20 cm (8 inch)
round cake tin and bake in a preheated
oven for 40–45 minutes until well risen
and firm to the touch. Turn out, take
off the paper and cool on a wire tray.
2. Make the fondant moulding paste.
Use one third to make one round tail,
2 eyes and a nose. Leave to set.
3. Take another piece of icing and
colour it orange; shape this into a
carrot. Colour a little food icing with
green food colouring and use to make
the carrot leaves. Press into position.
Colour the remaining icing pale blue
with a few drops of blue food
colouring, make a nose and 2 eyes, then
cut the remainder into 4 pieces.
4. Shape 2 pieces into back legs and 2
pieces into front feet.
5. Make up the butter cream and tint
pale blue. Colour two thirds of the
coconut pale blue and one third green
with the food colourings.
6. Cut the cake in half (see diagram
below) and sandwich together with
apricot glaze. Place the cake on the
board.
7. Brush the whole cake with apricot
glaze and press the legs and feet in
position. Using a palette knife, cover
the whole of the cake with blue butter
cream to coat evenly.
8. Cover the cake with blue coconut,
brushing the excess off the board.
Brush the remaining board with glaze
and sprinkle with green coconut.
9. Press the tail, eyes and nose on to
the face and highlight the eyes and nose
with the blue pen. Place the carrot in
position.
10. Cut 2 large ears (shaped as in
diagram below) and 6 thin whiskers
from the rice paper and place in
position.

Opposite: the completed
Bunny Big Ears about to eat a
nice juicy carrot

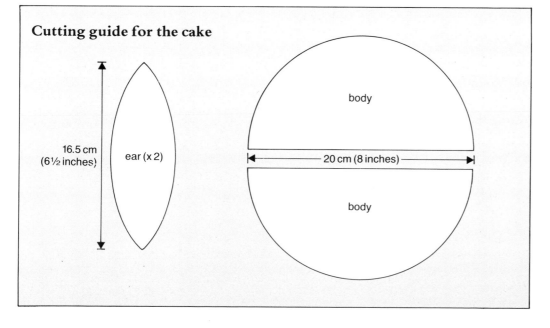

Cutting guide for the cake

16.5 cm
(6½ inches)

ear (x 2)

body

20 cm (8 inches)

body

Covering the cake board with coloured desiccated coconut to make the background

Making the clouds and sun in the sky behind Humpty Dumpty

Opposite: Humpty Dumpty sitting on a wall

HUMPTY DUMPTY

3-egg quantity Chocolate Quick Mix Cake mixture (pages 22-3)
1 quantity Butter Cream (page 38)
1 tablespoon cocoa powder
2 teaspoons boiling water
pink, blue, green and yellow food colourings
50 g (2 oz) desiccated coconut
4 tablespoons Apricot Glaze (page 30)
2 × 20 cm (8 inch) thin silver cake boards
25 g (1 oz) liquorice comfits
1 tablespoon chocolate flavour toasted rice
50 g (2 oz) Marzipan (page 30)
black food colouring pen
1 sheet rice paper

Preparation time: 40 minutes
Cooking time: 25-45 minutes
Oven: 170°C, 325°F, Gas Mark 3

1. Grease and base line a 1 litre (2 pint) pudding basin, an 18 cm (7 inch) round sandwich tin and a 500 g (1 lb) loaf tin.
2. Place 2 tablespoonsful of the cake mixture in the basin, and divide the remainder between the 2 tins.
3. Bake in a preheated oven for about 30 minutes for the basin and round cake, and 40-45 minutes for the loaf tin, until well risen and firm to the touch.
4. Turn out of the basin and tins and remove the paper; cool on a wire tray.
5. Make the butter cream and divide into 3 portions. Blend the cocoa and water together and cool, then beat it into one third of the butter cream icing. Colour another third of the icing pink and the remaining third blue with the appropriate food colourings.
6. Reserve 1 tablespoonful of coconut, divide the remainder into 3 and colour one third blue, one third green and one third yellow by adding a few drops of each food colouring to a portion of coconut and mixing until well blended.
7. Brush the cake board with apricot glaze and sprinkle over the coloured coconut to make a background picture (see pictures, left).

8. Spread the top and sides of the oblong cake with the chocolate butter cream icing, place on the cake board 1 cm (½ inch) from the bottom and mark the icing to resemble a brick wall.
9. Sandwich the round and pudding basin cakes together with apricot glaze and spread half with pink icing and half with blue icing. Place on the board against the top of the wall.
10. Arrange the sweets across the middle of the cake to form a 'belt', and also place the eyes, nose and mouth in position. Press the toasted rice in position for hair.
11. Colour half the marzipan pink and half blue with food colourings and shape the pink into arms and the blue into legs. Place in position on the cake.
12. The second cake board may be used, if liked, to add the Humpty Dumpty nursery rhyme to the cake. Brush a 7.5 mm (3 inch) border of apricot glaze on the board and sprinkle with tinted desiccated coconut. Use a food colouring pen to write the rhyme on the rice paper and secure it to the cake board, inside the coconut border, with a little glaze.

CHESS BOARD

1 × 20 cm (8 inch) square Light Fruit Cake (page 16)
25 cm (10 inch) square silver cake board
4 tablespoons Apricot Glaze (page 30)
750 g (1½ lb) Marzipan (page 30)
1½ quantities Fondant Moulding Paste (page 36)
brown and black food colourings

Preparation time: 1 hour plus setting
Cooking time: 2¾–3 hours (for cake)
Oven: 150°C, 300°F, Gas Mark 2

1. Place the cake on the board and trim the top if necessary to make it level. Brush the top and sides with apricot glaze, then cover with the marzipan. Trim, reserving the trimmings.
2. Make the fondant moulding paste. Divide the icing in half and colour one half brown with a few drops of brown food colouring. Leave the other half cream. Colour the remaining marzipan with black food colouring.
3. Roll out ⅔ of the brown paste thinly and cut into an oblong 20 × 10 cm (8 × 4 inches). Cut the oblong into 4 × 2.5 cm (1 inch) strips, then each strip into 8 squares making 32 in all. Knead the trimmings together and reserve.

4. Repeat with the cream moulding paste and leave until almost set.

5. Roll out and trim 2 cream and 2 brown strips of moulding paste the width and length of each side of the cake and place alternate strips around the sides. Brush the top of the cake with glaze. Arrange alternate squares of brown and cream moulding paste on top of the cake. Leave to set. Cut out a strip of brown and cream moulding paste to trim the top edge of the cake.

6. Make the chess men from black marzipan and the trimmings of the cream moulding paste. Leave to set, then arrange them on the appropriate squares on top of the cake.

Left: the Chess Board with chessmen laid out; right: four Playing Cards

PLAYING CARDS

2-egg quantity lemon Quick Mix Cake mixture (pages 22–3)
1 quantity Fondant Moulding Paste (page 36)
2 tablespoons Apricot Glaze (page 30)
red and black food colourings
red and black food colouring pens

Preparation time: 40 minutes
Cooking time: 25–30 minutes
Oven: 170°C, 325°F, Gas Mark 3

1. Bake the cake mixture in a greased and lined 28 × 18 cm (11 × 7 inch) oblong tin, 4 cm (1½ inches) deep in a preheated oven for 25–30 minutes until well risen and firm. Turn out, remove the paper and cool on a wire tray.
2. Make the fondant moulding paste.
3. Cut the cake into 4 pieces each 14 × 9 cm (5½ × 3½ inches) and trim. Brush the sides and top of each cake with some of the apricot glaze.
4. Cut the moulding paste into 4 pieces. Roll out each piece large enough to cover each cake, place them over, press in position and trim neatly to fit.
5. Knead the moulding paste trimmings together. Cut in half and colour one half red and the other black with a few drops of the food colourings.
6. Roll out the red moulding paste and cut out 8 hearts and 6 diamond shapes using a cutter or a template. Knead the trimmings together and re-roll, then cut out 8 thin strips.
7. Arrange the hearts and diamonds on to 2 of the cakes and use the thin strips to make a red border around the top and base of each. Secure with some of the apricot glaze. Using the red food-colouring pen, write the numbers '8' or '6' in the top and bottom opposite corners.
8. Repeat with the black icing, cutting out 5 clubs and 7 spades and 8 thin strips. Place in position on the remaining cakes, secured with the remaining glaze. Using the black food-colouring pen, write '5' or '7' in the top and bottom opposite corners.

LUNCH BOX AND FLASK

2-egg quantity Quick Mix Cake
  mixture (pages 22-3)
2-egg quantity Whisked Sponge Cake
  (pages 24-5)
1 quantity Butter Cream (page 38)
yellow, red and green food colourings
150 g (6 oz) Marzipan (page 30)
4 tablespoons Apricot Glaze (page 30)
25 cm (10 inch) square thin silver cake
  board
2 mini milk chocolate fudge bars

Preparation time: 50-60 minutes,
                     plus setting
Cooking time: 30-35 minutes
Oven: 170°C, 325°F, Gas
                     Mark 3

1. Place the Quick Mix cake mixture in a greased and lined 28 × 18 cm (11 × 7 inch) oblong tin, 4 cm (1½ inches) deep and bake in a preheated oven for 30-35 minutes until well risen and firm to the touch. Turn out, remove the paper and cool on a wire tray.

2. Place the Whisked Sponge Cake mixture in a greased and lined 28 × 18 cm (11 × 7 inch) Swiss roll tin and bake on a shelf just above the oblong cake for 10-15 minutes. Follow the instructions for making a Swiss roll on page 24.

3. Make the butter cream and colour it bright yellow with the yellow food colouring.

4. Knead some red food colouring into ⅔ of the marzipan until it is bright red. Colour the remaining marzipan a bright apple green.

5. Cut the oblong cake in half and sandwich together with apricot glaze, see the diagram below, and cut a 5 cm (2 inch) slice off the Swiss roll and discard (or eat).

6. Brush both cakes with apricot glaze and place on the cake board. Carefully spread the yellow butter cream smoothly and evenly over the oblong cake, using a palette knife dipped in hot water.

7. Coat the Swiss roll evenly the same way and stand it on end next to the oblong cake. Leave in a cool place to set.

8. Roll out a strip of red marzipan 4 cm (1½ inches) wide by 23 cm (9 inches) long. Carefully place around the top end of the Swiss roll and join carefully. Cut out a 6 cm (2½ inch) round of marzipan and place in position on top of the Swiss roll. Mould a small marzipan handle and leave to set.

9. Cut one of the fudge bars in half and cover the complete bar and the 2 pieces in red marzipan. Position as a handle on the lunch box using the 2 small pieces as handle supports.

10. Roll out the remaining red marzipan thinly and cut out 5 mm (¼ inch) strips. Use to trim the edges and base of the lunch box. Place a red strip of marzipan across the top and down the side of the lunch box and mark the opening line with a knife. Cut out the lock and the letters for the name of the child with an alphabet cutter. Using any patterned cutter, cut out some shapes and press in position on the lunch box and flask.

11. Attach the handle to the cup on the flask with glaze.

12. Mould an apple shape from the green marzipan, and decorate with a leaf made from a diamond-shaped piece of marzipan, its edges pressed into a leaf form, and with veins marked on.

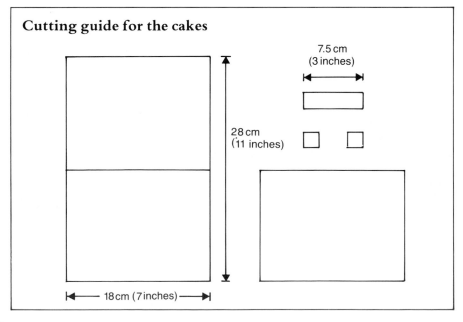

Cutting guide for the cakes

7.5 cm (3 inches)

28 cm (11 inches)

18 cm (7 inches)

The brightly coloured Lunch
Box and Flask with a green
marzipan apple

The Christmas Tree cake
decorated with a star and
chocolate balls wrapped in
coloured foil

CHRISTMAS TREE

Spicy Dough:
6 tablespoons golden syrup
50 g (2 oz) margarine
50 g (2 oz) light soft brown sugar
350 g (12 oz) plain flour
3 teaspoons ground allspice
1 teaspoon bicarbonate of soda
1 teaspoon water
1 (size 3) egg
1 quantity Fondant Moulding Paste
    (page 36)
green and gold food colourings
2 tablespoons Apricot Glaze (page 30)
2 tablespoons Royal Icing (page 32)
150 g (5 oz) milk chocolate balls in foil
    wrappers
icing sugar to dredge
18 cm (7 inch) cake board

Preparation time: 40 minutes, plus drying and setting
Cooking time: 10-15 minutes
Oven: 180°C, 350°F, Gas Mark 4

1. Place the syrup, margarine and sugar in a saucepan and heat gently until the margarine has melted. Remove from the heat.
2. Place the flour and allspice in a bowl. Mix the bicarbonate of soda and water together, then stir it into the flour with the egg and the melted margarine mixture.
3. Stir well with a wooden spoon to form a soft dough. Cover and leave for 5 minutes.
4. Line 2 baking sheets with non-stick silicone paper. Make a Christmas Tree template (see the diagram right).
5. Roll out a quarter of the dough on one of the lined baking sheets. Place the tree shape on top and carefully cut out and remove the excess dough.
6. Bake in a preheated oven for 10-15 minutes until risen and golden brown. Cool on the paper for 10 minutes, then remove and place on a cooling rack.
7. Repeat to make 4 tree cut-outs and a star (using a small star cutter or template). Use the excess dough for gingerbread boys and girls.

8. Make the fondant moulding paste. Reserve a small piece and tint the remainder of the icing green.
9. Brush each of the tree pieces with apricot glaze. Roll out a quarter of the moulding paste thinly. Place the tree shape on top, glazed side downwards, and cut around the shape. Leave to dry.
10. Repeat with the remaining 3 tree shapes; when the icing has dried, glaze and ice the other sides. Leave to dry.
11. Spread a thick layer of royal icing in the centre of the board to stand the tree on. Take one tree shape and press into the icing firmly, so that it stands upright.
12. Spread or pipe the royal icing along each straight edge of each tree shape and press them into the base icing, so that all the straight edges meet in the centre.
13. Press 4 small pieces of white icing between the tree trunks as supports. Tie a piece of thread underneath the top branches to secure the pieces together until the tree has set.
14. Cut out a white moulding paste star and attach to the biscuit star with a little apricot glaze. Paint with gold food colouring and leave to set.
15. Pipe a bead of icing on each branch and on the foil-wrapped chocolate balls, then carefully press alternate coloured balls into position. Place the star on top in the same way.
16. Dredge the board with icing sugar.

Cutting the fondant moulding paste to fit the tree piece; the tree has been brushed with apricot glaze before being laid, glaze side down, on the moulding paste

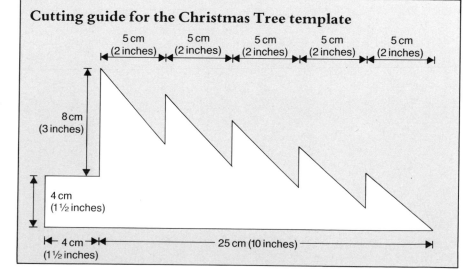

Cutting guide for the Christmas Tree template

5 cm (2 inches) | 5 cm (2 inches) | 5 cm (2 inches) | 5 cm (2 inches) | 5 cm (2 inches)

8 cm (3 inches)

4 cm (1½ inches)

4 cm (1½ inches)

25 cm (10 inches)

CIRCUS RING

2-egg quantity Quick Mix Cake
    mixture (pages 22-3)
½ quantity Fondant Moulding Paste
    (page 36)
red, yellow, green, blue, black and
    purple food colourings
25 cm (10 inch) thin round silver cake
    board
1 tablespoon Apricot Glaze (page 30)
3 tablespoons light soft brown sugar
2 candy sticks
1 piece strawberry flavour liquorice
8 edible circus wafers
1 clown, 2 elephants, 2 seals with balls,
    made from moulding icing (see
    method) or use bought figures

Preparation time: 1 hour, plus
                    setting
Cooking time: 35-40 minutes
Oven: 170°C, 325°F, Gas
                    Mark 3

1. Place the cake mixture in a greased
and base-lined 20 cm (8 inch) sandwich
tin and bake in a preheated oven for 35-
40 minutes until well risen and firm to
the touch. Turn out, remove the paper
and cool on a wire tray.
2. Make the fondant moulding paste.
Reserve one third and cut the
remaining two-thirds into 6 pieces.
Colour the pieces red, yellow, green
and blue with the food colourings.
Wrap each piece in cling film until
used.
3. Place the cake on the board and
brush it all over with apricot glaze.
Mark the cake on the outside edge into
8 equal sections.
4. Roll out and trim 2 pieces of red
moulding paste to fit 2 side sections of
the cake. Press one piece in position,
with the remaining piece on the
opposite side. Repeat with the blue,
yellow and green moulding paste, so
that the outside of the cake is covered in
alternating coloured sections.
5. Knead the trimmings together,
keeping the colours separate, then
mould each colour into 2 square-edge
lengths to fit each section. To do this,

make a roll from each colour then
flatten to make a four-sided shape.
6. Place the edging pieces around the
top edge of the cake, matching the side
colours.
7. Sprinkle the top of the cake with
sugar. Press the candy sticks into the
cake, one at each side. Cut a thin strip
of red liquorice and tie it around the
candy sticks to make a tight rope.

The clown and ball made from
multi-coloured fondant
moulding paste

An elephant and a seal made
from greyish-purple fondant
moulding paste and decorated
with coloured trimmings

8. Stick the circus wafers on to the outside of the cake, one on each of the coloured sections.

9. Mould the clown from multi-coloured moulding paste. To do this, take a piece of white paste the size of a walnut and press small balls of red, yellow, green and blue paste on to it. Roll gently to blend all the colours together and mould into a clown (see picture, opposite top).

10. Colour half the remaining white moulding paste greyish purple using black and purple food colouring. Mould 2 elephants, using coloured icing trimmings to make their hats.

11. Colour the reserved moulding paste black and use to make 2 seals and balls. Leave to set, then place the animals in the circus ring.

The completed Circus Ring makes a lively and colourful scene

SANTA IN THE CHIMNEY

3-egg quantity Quick Mix Cake
  mixture (pages 22-3)
1 quantity Fondant Moulding Paste
  (page 36)
red, brown, green and blue food
  colourings
2 tablespoons Apricot Glaze (page 30)
18 cm (7 inch) square cake board
brown food colouring pen
icing sugar to dredge (optional)

Preparation time: 45 minutes
Cooking time: 40-45 minutes
Oven: 170°C, 325°F, Gas
                  Mark 3

1. Place the cake mixture in a greased
and lined 28 × 18 cm (11 × 7 inch)
oblong tin 4 cm (1½ inches) deep.
Bake in a preheated oven for 40-45
minutes until well risen and firm to the
touch. Turn out, remove paper and
cool on a wire tray.
2. Make the fondant moulding paste.
Divide into 3 and colour one portion
red and one brown with a few drops of
food colouring.
3. Cut out the cake according to the
diagram right and sandwich the 2
squares together with apricot glaze.
Place on the board and brush the top
and sides with glaze.
4. Roll out the brown moulding paste
and trim to a strip as wide as the side of
the cake, and 50 cm (20 inches) long.
Carefully fit the paste around the side
of the cake and, using the point of a
knife, mark a brick pattern on each side
to form a chimney stack. Knead the
trimmings together.
5. Roll out the white moulding paste
and trim to a 15 cm (6 inch) square,
then leave to set. Knead the trimmings
together. Place in position on top of the
chimney stack.
6. Make a 7.5 cm (3 inch) ring about
2.5 cm (1 inch) deep from some of the
remaining brown moulding paste for
the chimney pot and place in position
on the top.
7. To make the Santa, use the 2 cut-out
cakes as the head and body. Knead a

piece of the brown into some of the
white moulding paste to make a flesh
colour for the face.
8. Roll out the flesh-coloured
moulding paste and use to cover the
head. Roll out the red moulding paste
and use part to cover the body and part
to make a cloak. Cover the body with
the red moulding paste and place the
head on top, securing with glaze. Make
a beard, hair and eyebrows from some
white moulding paste. Colour a piece
of white paste blue and make 2 tiny
eyes. Secure the pieces on the cake with
a little glaze.
9. Cover the head and body with the
cloak and trim the edge with white
moulding paste.
10. Place the Santa into the chimney
pot, tucking in the surplus paste.
11. To make the sack, roll out the
remaining brown paste and wrap it
round a small piece of remaining cake.
Draw it together at the top and press.
Make a few small shapes from red, blue
and green paste for the parcels.
12. Tie the sack with white paste and
place on top of the chimney with the
parcels in the top of the sack.

Pieces of red and white
fondant moulding paste
shaped ready for assembling
into Santa and his cloak

Opposite: Santa and his sack
of toys in the chimney

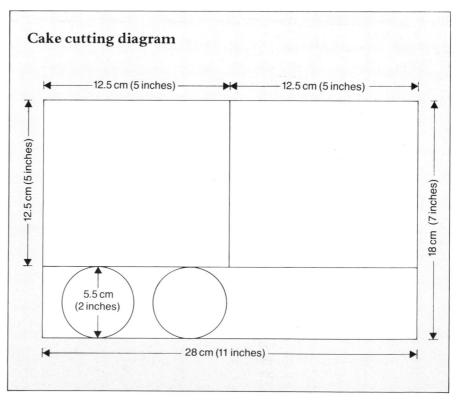

Cake cutting diagram

12.5 cm (5 inches)   12.5 cm (5 inches)

12.5 cm (5 inches)

18 cm (7 inches)

5.5 cm
(2 inches)

28 cm (11 inches)

The green and brown marzipan used to make Joseph, with (right) the completed figure

A donkey and lamb shaped from coloured marzipan. The lamb's face made with a food-colouring pen, the donkey's with marzipan trimmings

NATIVITY SCENE

1 quantity Spicy Dough, see Christmas Tree (page 125)
2 tablespoons Royal Icing (page 32)
25 cm (10 inch) thin round silver cake board
4 shredded wheat
250 g (8 oz) Marzipan (pages 30-1)
blue, green, brown and yellow food colourings
100 g (4 oz) Fondant Moulding Paste (page 36)
brown edible food colouring pen

Preparation time: 1 hour, plus cooling
Cooking time: 10-15 minutes
Oven: 180°C, 350°F, Gas Mark 4

1. Make the Spicy Dough according to the instructions (page 125) for the Christmas Tree. Cut out the templates following the diagram below.
2. Roll out the dough thinly and, using the templates, cut out the roof and back of the stable, the side pieces and the doors and the crib pieces. Use a shaped cutter to cut out a star.
3. Place the pieces on baking sheets lined with non-stick silicone paper. Mark lines with a knife on to each piece of dough and place a thin strip of dough across each door piece.

4. Bake in a preheated oven for 10-15 minutes until well risen and golden brown. Cool on the paper, then transfer to a wire tray.
5. Make the royal icing. Assemble the stable by spreading or piping the edges of each piece with icing and pressing them together. Secure the doors with icing. Place on the cake board.
6. Assemble the crib and secure the pieces with icing. Crush 1 shredded wheat and sprinkle over the floor of the stable. Carefully split the remaining shredded wheats into half, making 6 pieces, and place them in position on the roof.
7. Cut the marzipan into 4 pieces. Colour one piece green, one blue, one brown and one flesh-coloured (with pink and a dot of brown), using the food colourings.
8. Cut off 2 pieces of fondant moulding paste and colour one piece yellow and the other pale flesh colour. Wrap each in cling film.
9. To model each of the figures, use white moulding paste to make the baby's cover and the angels' bodies, hands and heads, flesh colour for the baby's head and body and yellow for the halos and wings. Place the pieces together and secure with a little icing. Cut out a yellow moulding paste star to cover the gingerbread star. Place in position on the stable roof.

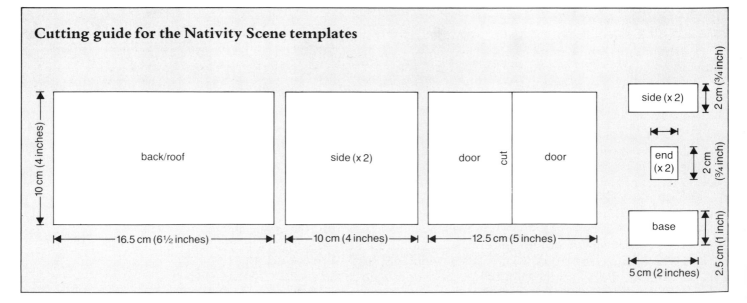

Cutting guide for the Nativity Scene templates

back/roof
10 cm (4 inches)
16.5 cm (6½ inches)

side (x 2)
10 cm (4 inches)

door | cut | door
12.5 cm (5 inches)

side (x 2)
2 cm (¾ inch)

end (x 2)
2 cm (¾ inch)

base
2.5 cm (1 inch)
5 cm (2 inches)

10. Make Mary's body out of blue marzipan and the head and hands from flesh-coloured moulding paste. Make some light brown hair and mould the head-dress from white moulding paste. Assemble the figure as above.

11. Using brown marzipan, model Joseph's beard, hair and crook. Make his head and hands from flesh coloured and his body, collar and sleeves from green marzipan. Assemble the figure.

12. Make the donkey from the remaining brown and flesh-coloured marzipan. Shape a lamb from white marzipan.

13. Mark all the features in with edible food colouring pens or with tiny pieces of moulding paste or marzipan. Place the figures around the stable with the baby in the crib.

The Nativity Scene, with Mary, Joseph, angels and animals surrounding the crib

Small Cakes

This chapter includes an interesting variety of small cakes, tartlets, biscuits and petits fours. Simple sponge cakes, biscuit recipes and pastry are all turned into works of art with the use of colourings, icings, fillings, chocolate, fruit and flowers. The recipes are easy to follow, so even inexperienced cooks will produce beautifully decorated cakes.

The novelty cakes are made from basic quick mix recipes and turned into dice using coloured marzipan and fondant moulding paste, or chocolate boxes using milk and plain chocolate. For these recipes, the squares must be measured carefully before cutting, and the pieces handled as little as possible.

Sponge fish are easily decorated if you use a plain piping nozzle to cut out the round scales, about 10 at a time.

The flower pot cakes are baked in petit four cases and spread with chocolate; make holes in the top with a skewer before fitting the angelica stems in position.

Try the Animal biscuits and Christmas tree cookies before making the novelty cakes based on the same dough. These recipes can be decorated in your own style and colours, and wrapped in cling film to keep fresh.

When making and colouring the marzipan for petits fours, be careful not to over-knead it as it may become oily and difficult to mould.

Pastry tartlets or boats can be made ahead of time. Once the moulds have been lined with pastry, stack them together and chill until firm, or overnight. Keep a careful watch while baking them as sweet pastry cooks quickly. Tap the mould to remove the pastry cases when they have cooled slightly. Fill the pastry cases on the day they are to be used.

Chocolate cases can be made from melted plain or milk chocolate. Fill and brush one case at a time, thickly covering the inside of the paper case. If the chocolate hardens before it is used, simply re-melt it over hot water. Once the chocolate has set, carefully peel the paper case away from the chocolate at the top and work towards the base.

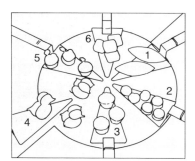

1. Mocha Boats filled with a rum and chocolate cream
2. Petits fours made from tinted and shaped marzipan
3. Chocolate Truffle Cups filled with swirls of rum-flavoured chocolate cream
4. Pale yellow meringue chicks sit on large chocolate buttons
5. Flower Pot Cakes made from the Quick Mix Cake mixture and decorated with chocolate and sugar flowers
6. Square marzipan petits fours

Top left: Christmas Tree Cookies; top right: Goldfish Cakes; bottom: Chocolate Truffle Cups

CHRISTMAS TREE COOKIES

Makes 25

Biscuit dough:
150 g (5 oz) plain flour
25 g (1 oz) custard powder
½ teaspoon baking powder
75 g (3 oz) caster sugar
75 g (3 oz) butter
1 egg (size 3), separated

Decoration:
red, green, yellow and orange food
   colourings
225 g (8 oz) thin fruit-flavoured boiled
   sweets (assorted colours)

Preparation time: about 20 minutes
Cooking time: 10 minutes
Oven: 180°C, 350°F, Gas
                      Mark 4

Keeping the cookies
These brightly coloured edible decorations for the Christmas tree will keep for up to 4 weeks if covered in cling film before being hung on the tree. Otherwise they will keep for about 2 weeks.

1. Place the flour, custard powder, baking powder and sugar in a mixing bowl. Add the butter, cut into small pieces, and rub in finely with the fingers until the mixture resembles breadcrumbs.
2. Stir in the egg yolk and half of the white and mix with a fork to form a soft dough. Knead on a lightly floured surface until smooth.
3. Line 2 baking sheets with non-stick silicone paper. Roll out the dough thinly and cut out various shapes using round or square fluted cutters between 4 cm (2 inches) and 7½ cm (3 inches) in size.
4. Place the shapes a little apart on the prepared baking sheets, then cut out the centres with smaller cutters shaped, for example, in hearts, rounds, Christmas trees and bells. Remove the centre shape and place on another baking sheet, or knead together to make more full-size shapes and cut out as before.

5. Divide the remainder of the egg white into 4 portions and colour each portion with a few drops of food colouring, so that the egg glazes are red, green, yellow and orange.
6. Using a fine paint brush, paint the frame of each dough shape with different coloured egg glaze. Place a matching fruit sweet in the centre of each shape. If the sweets are too large, cut them in half and place one half in each shape. Make a hole at the top of each shape with a skewer. Paint the centre cut-out pieces if using.
7. Place the baking sheets in a preheated oven in the centre and just below and bake for about 10 minutes, until the sweets have melted and filled the space and the biscuits are set.
8. Leave the biscuits to cool on the paper, then peel off carefully when completely set. Thread a piece of coloured twine through the holes and tie on to the Christmas tree. The small centre pieces can be packed in a glass jar or pretty box.

GOLDFISH CAKES

Makes 15

50 g (2 oz) Quick Mix Cake mixture (pages 22-3)
3 tablespoons Apricot Glaze (page 30)
3 tablespoons hundreds and thousands
orange food colouring
175 g (6 oz) Marzipan (pages 30-1)
cornflour

Preparation time: 15 minutes
Cooking time: 15 minutes
Oven: 160°C, 325°F, Gas Mark 3

1. Grease 15 boat moulds. Divide the cake mixture among them and bake in a preheated oven for about 15 minutes until well risen and firm to touch. Turn out at once on to a wire tray to cool.
2. Brush the underneath of each sponge shape with the apricot glaze and just the pointed end of the flat top. Dip the shapes in hundreds and thousands to coat the glazed area.

3. Knead a few drops of food colouring into the marzipan to colour orange. Roll out very thinly on a lightly cornfloured surface.
4. Using a 1 cm (½ inch) plain nozzle, cut out lots of rounds for the fishes scales, then cut out 15 'V' shapes for the tails and 15 rounds for the eyes.
5. Carefully brush the plain sponge with apricot glaze and place the eyes on the hundreds and thousands and the tails at the opposite ends. Arrange the scales overlapping from tail to head.

CHOCOLATE TRUFFLE CUPS

Makes 18

100 g (4 oz) milk chocolate, melted (page 140)
100 g (4 oz) plain chocolate
40 g (1½ oz) unsalted butter
1 tablespoon single cream
1-2 tablespoons dark rum or sherry
6 pistachio nuts, skinned and chopped

Preparation time: 15 minutes, plus setting

1. Place 18 mini paper cake cases on a baking sheet. Place half a teaspoonful of melted milk chocolate into one paper case. Using a small brush, spread the chocolate evenly up the side and over the base of the paper case. Repeat to coat the remaining paper cases, using up all the milk chocolate. Leave in the refrigerator or a cool place to set hard.
2. Place the plain chocolate and butter in a bowl over a saucepan of hot water off the heat, stirring occasionally until melted. Stir in the cream and rum until well blended. Remove from the bowl of hot water and leave to cool, giving an occasional stir, until the mixture peaks softly.
3. Place the chocolate in a piping bag fitted with a medium star tube and pipe a swirl of mixture into each chocolate case. Sprinkle with chopped nuts and leave to set. Carefully peel off the paper cases and arrange on a serving plate.

Chocolate Truffle Cups
Brush the paper cases evenly with a thick layer of chocolate, making sure there are no gaps or weak places. Leave them to set hard in a refrigerator or cool place. Peel the paper case carefully away from the top edge first, then work down to the base to prevent the truffle cups cracking.

SPONGE DICE

Makes 16

100 g (4 oz) quantity Chocolate Quick
    Mix Cake mixture (pages 22-3)
227 g (8 oz) Fondant Moulding Paste
    (page 36)
red and green food colourings
250 g (8 oz) Marzipan (pages 30-1)
6 tablespoons Apricot Glaze (page 30)
cornflour

Preparation time: 30 minutes
Cooking time: 35-40 minutes
Oven: 160°C, 325°F, Gas
                    Mark 3

1. Cook the cake mixture in a greased,
greaseproof paper-lined 18 cm (7 inch)
square tin for 35-40 minutes, until well
risen and firm to the touch. Turn out,
remove the paper and cool the cake on
a wire tray.
2. Cut off a small piece of the fondant
moulding paste the size of a walnut and
reserve. Colour the remaining
moulding paste red with a few drops of
red food colouring. Knead a few drops
of green food colouring into the
marzipan until evenly coloured green.
3. Trim and cut the cake into 16, 4 cm
(1½ inch) squares and brush evenly
with apricot glaze.
4. Roll out the red moulding paste
thinly on a surface sprinkled with
cornflour and cut out 40, 4 cm
(1½ inch) squares, re-rolling the
trimmings when necessary. Stick the
moulding paste squares on to the sides
and tops of 8 cakes, pressing the joins
together.
5. Repeat with the marzipan, cutting
out the squares to cover the remaining
8 cakes.
6. Use the reserved white moulding
paste to roll into tiny dots, and secure
one to six dots on each side of the cakes
using a little apricot glaze, to make 16
dice.

YELLOW CHICKS

Makes 16

2 egg whites
100 g (4 oz) caster sugar
yellow food colouring
liquorice food colouring pen
150 ml (¼ pint) double or whipping
    cream
2 teaspoons grated lemon rind
10 large chocolate buttons

Preparation time: 20 minutes
Cooking time: 2 hours
Oven: 100°C, 200°F, Gas
                    Mark ¼

1. Line 2 baking sheets with non-stick
silicone paper. Place the egg whites in a
bowl and whisk until stiff. Gradually
whisk in the sugar until the mixture
stands up in peaks.
2. Add a few drops of food colouring
to the meringue to colour it pale
yellow.
3. Place the mixture in a piping bag
fitted with a 1 cm (½ inch) plain
nozzle. Pipe a small round of the
mixture about 2 cm (1 inch) in
diameter on to the baking sheet for the
body and pull off to the right to form a
wing. Pipe a smaller round above and
pull off to the left for the beak. This
makes one half chick. Pipe another half
chick with the wing to the left and the
beak to the right.
4. Repeat to pipe another 15 left hand
chicks and 15 right hand chicks. Place
in a preheated oven as near to the centre
as possible and cook for about 2 hours,
or until the meringue chicks lift easily
off the paper.
5. Using a fine paint brush and some
yellow colouring, paint the beak and
wing markings on to each chick. Mark
in the eyes with the food colouring
pen.
6. Place the cream and lemon rind in a
bowl and whip until thick. Spread half
of the chicks with most of the cream
leaving a small amount and sandwich
together with the matching half.
7. Sit each chick on a chocolate button
secured with a little cream.

Making meringues
Always use 2-3 day old
egg whites if possible
when making meringues
as they dry out more
quickly. Also make sure
the sugar is whisked well
into the egg whites a
little at a time, ensuring a
light fluffy meringue.
Dry in a cool oven until
the meringues lift easily
off the paper, and store
in a dry place in an
airtight container.

ANIMAL BISCUITS

Makes 25

150 g (5 oz) plain flour
50 g (2 oz) ground rice
75 g (3 oz) caster sugar
150 g (5 oz) soft margarine
1 teaspoon vanilla essence
1 egg, separated
red, yellow and green food colourings
currants

Preparation time: about 15 minutes
Cooking time: 10-12 minutes
Oven: 180°C, 350°F, Gas
                      Mark 4

1. Place the flour, ground rice, caster sugar, margarine, vanilla essence and egg white into a mixing bowl. Mix together with a wooden spoon until the mixture begins to bind together, then knead it with the fingers until the mixture forms a soft dough.

2. Roll out thinly on a lightly floured surface. Using different shaped animal cutters, cut out the dough and place the shapes on lightly floured baking sheets.

3. Divide the egg yolk into 3 portions and colour each portion with a few drops of food colouring so that the egg glazes are red, yellow and green.

4. To decorate the animal shapes, brush on either stripes or dots of different egg glaze colours, or just paint on one plain colour. Make the animals' features with currants.

5. Place the baking sheets in a preheated oven on the centre shelf and just below and bake for 10-12 minutes until pale at the edges.

6. Cool for a few minutes, then remove carefully and place on a wire tray to cool.

From the left: Yellow Chicks, Sponge Dice, Animal Biscuits

137

PRALINE JAP CAKES

Makes 18

Japonaise mixture:
50 g (2 oz) ground almonds
25 g (1 oz) cornflour
75 g (3 oz) caster sugar
2 egg whites (size 3)
Praline:
100 g (4 oz) sugar
4 tablespoons water
75 g (3 oz) hazelnuts
Filling:
1 quantity Continental Butter Cream
   (pages 38-9)

Preparation time: 25 minutes, plus chilling
Cooking time: 30-35 minutes
Oven: 160°C, 325°F, Gas Mark 3

1. Line 2 baking sheets with non-stick silicone paper and mark 18, 4 cm (1½ inch) circles on each sheet of paper.
2. To make the japonaises, mix the almonds, cornflour and half of the sugar together in a bowl. Whisk the egg whites until stiff in another bowl, then whisk in the remaining sugar until the mixture peaks. Add the almond mixture and fold in carefully and well.
3. Place the mixture in a piping bag fitted with a 5 mm (¼ inch) plain tube. Pipe a spiral of the mixture from the centre to the edge of each marked circle.
4. Place the baking sheets in a preheated oven just above and just below the centre and bake for 30-35 minutes until lightly browned. Cool on the baking sheets; remove when cold.
5. To make the praline, cover a board with foil and grease lightly. Place the sugar and water in a saucepan, heat gently, stirring occasionally, until the sugar has dissolved. Add the nuts and boil rapidly until the mixture turns a golden brown. Remove 18 individual nuts and place apart on the foil. Pour the rest on the foil and leave until the praline is cold.
6. Reserve the whole nuts and finely blend the remaining caramel and nuts in a food processor to make ground praline. Turn out on a piece of greaseproof or waxed paper.
7. Use a little Continental Butter Cream to sandwich the japonaise rounds together. Spread the rest smoothly over each cake and chill until firm.
8. Coat each cake in the ground praline to cover evenly, then place a whole caramelled nut on top of each.

APRICOT CHOCOLATE BOXES

Makes 16

2 egg quantity Chocolate Whisked
   Sponge Cake mixture (pages 24-5)
150 g (5 oz) dried apricots, presoaked
   and drained
125 ml (¼ pint) water
125 ml (¼ pint) double cream
150 g (6 oz) plain chocolate, melted
150 g (6 oz) milk chocolate, melted
3 tablespoons Apricot Glaze (page 30)
16 small orange flowers, sugar-frosted
   (page 87)

Preparation time: 20 minutes, plus soaking
Cooking time: 25-30 minutes
Oven: 180°C, 350°F, Gas Mark 4

1. Cook the cake mixture in a greased, greaseproof paper-lined 18 cm (7 inch) square cake tin for 25-30 minutes until well risen and firm to touch. Turn out, remove paper and cool on a wire tray.
2. Place the apricots and water in a saucepan and bring to the boil. Cover and cook gently for 15-20 minutes or until tender. Leave until cold.
3. Place the apricots, juice and cream in a food processor or liquidizer and process until smooth. Set aside.
4. Cover 2 baking sheets with foil and grease lightly. Using a palette knife, spread plain chocolate thinly over one baking sheet into a square shape about 25 cm (10 inch) wide. Repeat with the milk chocolate. Leave until just set.
5. Using a sharp knife, mark the milk

Praline Jap Cakes
If the caramel sets hard in the saucepan, add a teaspoon of water and place the saucepan over a gentle heat. Do not stir, just allow the caramel to melt.

To coat the jap cakes, place the praline on to a piece of greaseproof paper. Place the iced jap cake in the centre and roll in the praline until evenly coated on every side.

Opposite, from the top:
Praline Jap Cakes, Apricot
Chocolate Boxes, Flower Pot
Cakes

chocolate carefully and cut into 40, 4 cm (1½ inch) squares. Mark and cut the plain chocolate into 40 4½ cm (1¾ inches) by 4 cm (1½ inches). Carefully peel off the foil.

6. Cut and trim the cake into 16, 4 cm (1½ inch) squares and brush each with apricot glaze. Stick 2 plain and 2 milk chocolate squares on to each cake to form a box. Fill each with apricot cream filling and decorate with a flower. Put a chocolate lid on each box, resting on the flower.

FLOWER POT CAKES

Makes 24

50 g (2 oz) Quick Mix Cake mixture
    (page 22-3)
50 g (2 oz) milk chocolate
2 teaspoons milk
25 g (1 oz) angelica
48 small sugar flowers

Preparation time:	20 minutes, plus cooling and setting
Cooking time:	15-20 minutes
Oven:	160°C, 325°F, Gas Mark 3

1. Cook the cake mixture in 24 mini paper cake cases for 15-20 minutes until well risen and firm. Cool on a wire tray.
2. Place the chocolate and milk in a bowl over a saucepan of hot water off the heat. Stir occasionally until the chocolate has melted and blended smoothly with the milk.
3. .Spread the top of each cake with a layer of chocolate. Keep back a little of the chocolate for later. Leave to set.
4. Cut two-thirds of the angelica into 24, 4 cm (1½ inch) strips for the stems and the remainder into small diamond shapes for leaves.
5. Use a skewer to make 2 holes in the centre of each cake. Cut ⅓ off each angelica stem and place a long and short stem into each cake, and 2 'leaves' at the base of each stem.
6. Secure the sugar flowers to the stems with a little melted chocolate.

Lining Fluted Tartlet Tins

Roll out the pastry thinly and use a plain cutter a size larger than the top of the tins. Cut out the pastry rounds and ease into each tartlet tin. Press into the base and up the sides, then trim off the excess pastry with a knife. Prick the bases, stack the tins together and chill thoroughly before baking.

How to melt chocolate

Half-fill a small saucepan with water and bring to the boil, then remove from the heat. Break up the chocolate and place in a dry, heat-proof bowl over the saucepan of water. Ensure the base of the bowl does not touch the water. Stir occasionally until the chocolate has melted, then use immediately.

LIME AND LEMON TARTLETS

Makes 16

1 quantity Sweet Pastry (see below)
Filling and topping:
150 ml (¼ pint) double cream
2 teaspoons grated lime rind
100 g (4 oz) icing sugar, sieved
1 tablespoon lemon juice
2 teaspoons grated lemon rind
To decorate:
thin strips of lime and lemon rind

Preparation time: 20 minutes, plus chilling
Cooking time: 10-15 minutes
Oven: 200°C, 400°F, Gas Mark 6

1. Make the pastry cases using 5 cm (2 inch) fluted tartlet tins and bake blind following the recipe below.
2. Place the cream and lime rind in a bowl and whip until thick. Fill each tartlet with lime cream and level the top. Chill for 10 minutes.
3. Mix together in a bowl the icing sugar, lemon juice and rind. Add a little boiling water until the icing has the consistency of thick cream.
4. Spread the top of each tartlet with a thin layer of lemon icing. Leave to set.
5. Cut out shapes of lime and lemon rind using a tiny cutter. Arrange a few shapes on each tartlet before serving.

MOCHA BOATS

Makes 16

Sweet pastry:
175 g (6 oz) plain flour
100 g (4 oz) butter, cut into small pieces
1 tablespoon caster sugar
1 egg yolk
Filling:
75 g (3 oz) plain chocolate, melted
1 egg, separated
3 teaspoons strong black coffee
150 ml (¼ pint) double or whipping cream

Preparation time: 20 minutes, plus chilling and setting
Cooking time: 10-15 minutes
Oven: 200°C, 400°F, Gas Mark 6

1. To make the pastry, place the flour in a bowl, add the butter and rub in finely with the fingers until the mixture resembles breadcrumbs.
2. Stir in the sugar, egg yolk and a little cold water if necessary and mix with a fork to form a firm dough. Knead on a lightly floured surface until smooth.
3. Place 10 boat moulds on a baking sheet. Roll out the pastry thinly and place on top of the boats. Ease the pastry into each boat, then roll across the tops with a rolling pin to remove excess pastry.
4. Press the pastry gently into each boat shape and prick with a fork. Knead the trimmings together and re-roll to line another 6 boat moulds. Chill for about 30 minutes or until firm.
5. Bake the pastry boats in a preheated oven just above centre for 10-15 minutes until lightly browned.
6. Invert the boat moulds on to a wire tray and remove carefully. Leave the pastry boats to cool.
7. Draw a design 16 times on a piece of waxed paper. Secure the paper to a board with sticky tape.
8. Place a tablespoonful of melted chocolate into a greaseproof paper piping bag, fold down the top and snip the point off the end. Pipe a thread of chocolate around each shape and leave to set hard.
9. To make the filling, stir the egg yolk and coffee into the remaining chocolate. Stiffly whisk the egg white and fold into the mixture until evenly mixed.
10. Fill each pastry boat with mocha filling and leave to set. Whip the cream until it peaks and place in a piping bag fitted with a small star tube.
11. Pipe coils of cream down the length of each boat, carefully remove the chocolate designs from the paper and use to decorate each boat.

From the left: Lime and
Lemon Tartlets, Marzipan
Petits Fours, Mocha Boats

MARZIPAN PETITS FOURS

Makes about 30

225 g (8 oz) White Marzipan (page 31)
pink and green food colourings
caster sugar for sprinkling
1 tablespoon melted chocolate (page 140)
12 hazelnuts

Preparation time: 30 minutes, plus setting

1. Cut the marzipan into 3 even-sized pieces. Add a drop of pink colouring to one piece and knead until evenly coloured. Add a drop of green colouring to another piece of marzipan and knead well.
2. Cut each piece of marzipan into 3 pieces. Roll out one piece of white marzipan on a lightly sugared surface and trim to a 10 cm (4 inch) square. Roll out a piece of green marzipan into a 20 cm (8 inch) long, thin pencil shape. Repeat with a piece of pink marzipan.
3. Cut each length in half and arrange a green and pink together on the white marzipan, and a pink and green on top. Bring the white marzipan over the colours and enclose, sealing well. Shape into a square-edge like a 'Battenberg'. Leave to set.
4. Take a piece of each colour and roll into long thin lengths. Plait the 3 colours together and cut into 10 pieces. Tuck the ends of each under to make them round. Dip the bases of each into melted chocolate and place on a piece of non-stick silicone paper to set.
5. Shape the remaining pieces of marzipan into short rolls. Cut each into 4 slices and place a hazelnut on top of each. Place the marzipan rounds under a preheated hot grill for 1 minute, or until lightly browned. Leave to cool.
6. Slice the Battenberg shape into about 10 slices and place all the marzipan petits fours into mini paper cases, if liked.

Index

Useful Addresses

These specialist shops can supply many of the cake decorating items and materials mentioned in this book.

Baker Smith (Cake Decorators) Ltd
The School of Cake Decorating
65 The Street
Tongham
Farnham
Surrey GU10 1DE
Tel: Runfold (025 18) 2984

Cake Decor
6 The Arcade
Worthing
West Sussex BN13 4RS
Tel: Worthing (0903) 39215

Cake Makers Boutique
28a Wood End Gardens
Northolt
Middlesex UB5 4JL
Tel: (01) 423 6886

Cakecraft Artistry & Sundries
(personal shoppers only)
54 Hazelwick Road
Three Bridges
Crawley
Sussex RH10 1LZ
Tel: Crawley (0293) 20875

Cookcraft Club Ltd
20 Canterbury Road
Herne Bay
Kent CT6 5EJ
Tel: Herne Bay (0227) 373049
Open Mon, Wed, Sat 10–4

F. & P. Catering Services Ltd
81 Hoe Street
Walthamstow
London E17 4SA
Tel: (01) 520 0893/0525

Homebakers Supplies
157–159 High Street
Wolstanton
Newcastle
Staffs ST5 0EJ
Tel: Wolstanton (0782) 614119

Items
72 Godstone Road
Kenley
Surrey CR2 5AA
Tel: (01) 668 0251
Closed Wednesday

Mary Ford Cake Artistry Centre
28–30 Southbourne Grove
Southbourne
Bournemouth
Dorset BH6 3RA
Tel: Bournemouth (0202) 431001/2

B. R. Mathews & Son
12 Gipsy Hill
Upper Norwood
London SE19 1NN
Tel: (01) 670 0788

West Midlands Cake Icing Centre
10 Moat Lane
Great Wyrley
Nr. Walsall
West Midlands WS6 6DU
Tel: Cheslyn Hay (0922) 410040

Wilson's Sugarcraft
10 Park Street
Horsham
West Sussex RH12 1DG
Tel: Horsham (0403) 60522

Woodnutt's
97 Church Road
Hove
Brighton
Sussex BN3 2BA
Tel: Brighton (0273) 738840

Acknowledgments

Photography: Clive Streeter

Photographic styling: Hilary Guy

Food prepared for photography by Rosemary Wadey and Janice Murfitt